Caught Between the Bettys

a memoir

Alice Borodkin

NEMO PUBLISHING

Caught Between the Bettys: a memoir
by Alice Borodkin

© 2015 Alice Borodkin

All rights reserved.

Editor: Barbara Munson, Munson Communications Editorial Services
Cover and Interior Design: Nick Zelinger, NZ Graphics

Photo of Betty Friedan (following page), courtesy of Wikimedia.com
Photo of *Betty Crocker's Cook Book for Boys and Girls* (following page),
courtesy of Wikimedia.com
Photo of 20th Century Limited, page 19, courtesy of Rickyrab, Wikimedia.com

ISBN: 978-0-9966877-0-6

Library of Congress Cataloging in Publication Data on file

Published by

NEMO PUBLISHING

First edition

Printed in the United States

Dedicated to The Bettys...

Most people think of a cookbook when they hear the name Betty Crocker. Or they picture this sweet, old-fashioned smiling woman who shows you how to maneuver your way around meal preparation. Recipes! Glorious presentations! Pleasing your man! Back when she was first introduced, we girls wanted to be like her. We believed, if you can bake perfect chocolate drop quickies while getting the house clean, the laundry done, the kids off to school, the martini ready for the hubby...baby, you got it made! Thanks, Betty C., for your role in this book.

Then along came Betty Friedan, no shrinking violet, who wrote a "simple handbook"—*The Feminine Mystique*—and shook up the world. She too lives on—in her courageous words that opened doors and in her crusade for equality for the sexes. If it hadn't been for this Betty, I'd probably have ended up an unfulfilled woman.

Contents

Prologue

It's 6:30 on a wet, wet, rainy night in June 1951. A real East Coast storm, with howling wind ripping through the trees, sheets of rain blowing sideways, thunder and lightning.

"Ally," husband of two weeks says on the phone, calling from what sounds like a wind-tossed phone booth, "can you pick me up at the subway? I'm drenched!"

"Sure," the Good Wife says, "I'm on the way!"

Ten minutes later I pull up at the subway station and Mr. Wonderful jumps around the car to the driver's side and says, "Move over, honey, I'll drive."

Honey looks at him like he is nuts. Move over?

"Get in," I say.

"No," he says as rain drips off his nose. "Move over, honey, and I'll drive home."

Honey is getting hot under the collar.

"I've been driving since I was thirteen, I have a license just like you do, and get in before you drown!" I yell over the wind and rain.

Once more, "Move over please, Alice." Now he is hot under the collar!

"Get in or I'm leaving," says the Good Wife, Honey, Alice.

No? Goodbye, and off Honey drives to my little nest, my big glass of wine, and the stone in my stomach thinking about what I had just done.

A bit later husband is home as he gets out of his mother's car. Just like a man, his Mommy saved him from drowning.

New husband probably recalculated his idea of the Good Wife.

1

Divas Are Born, Not Made

Alice, 1939

I come from a generation of divas. Back in the 1940s and 50s, divas were classy women, perhaps a bit full of themselves, who wore glamorous dresses, with their hair piled high on their heads or fashioned into a chignon held in place with tortoise-shell hairpins. Their nails and lips were often painted bright red. They never went anywhere without gloves. Most did not go to college—who needed college back then if you were a woman? Your job was to find the right man!

Divas are part and parcel of the times I come from. I grew up during World War II, and remember blackouts and rationing, men and women in uniform, Rosie the Riveter, war bond rallies and what seemed to a young girl to be the excitement of a world at war.

In those days, men and women were expected to adhere to certain roles. The men had theirs as the proud protectors and providers of their families and the women had theirs as housewives and mothers who relied solely on their men as breadwinners. Both played their parts well, if only on the surface.

When I married in the 1950s, I tried to follow all the rules: make your man happy, keep a clean home and prepare wonderful meals a la Betty Crocker. What I never counted on was the other Betty coming along: Betty Friedan. With the publication of *The Feminine Mystique*, I was now caught between the two Bettys. Thanks to Betty Friedan, I realized I wanted to do more with my life and be validated for what I was doing. I didn't know I was bucking the system, but as I think about it now, I sure was.

Betty Friedan was one of the first feminists to write about "The Problem Without a Name" in her 1964 book. How many of us lived through that period of time—after the war and before women's lib became a household term—and remember it today? We were the ones who questioned the difference between ironing your husband's shorts and what happened to my college degree?

Now we asked ourselves, "Am I supposed to be happy? What's wrong with me? I have 2.5 children, my spotless split-level in the suburbs; I am the perfect wife and mother." Along with many other women, I had been following *The Good Wife Book*. Yes, it was a real book given to me at my wedding shower. But *The Good Wife Book* had told us to abdicate our power, what little we had, and give most of it over to our new husbands. We did.

———

This is my memoir, with few revelations for those of us in my era (but maybe lots of *Oh, yeahs! Been there, done that!*) and it also is a history lesson and cautionary tale for the next generations. If you don't remember the time when newspaper classified job ads were separated out as "Men Wanted" and "Women Wanted," with the women's qualifications described as "Must be attractive"...and you assume women have always had access to reproductive rights... here is your chance to learn what it was really like "back then." After all, if you don't know where you came from, how can you know where you're going?

I like to say I am writing this memoir because I went to sleep when I was 12 and woke up when I was 80! Never too old for an awakening!

So here I am, older and wiser, after the housewife and mother role, still bucking the system and the cultural mores of the late 1940s and 50s. This rebellion had always seemed to come naturally to me as the tornado in my soul told me I was worth more...I simply wanted to be recognized for who I was and what I could do. Now, in 2015, my crusade isn't the battle of the sexes, it's human rights that's my fight.

This is my story of how I struggled with my role in life from the beginning. I just had a gut feeling I could, should and wanted to be doing more. Like many other women of that time, in the beginning, I buried those urges in favor of motherhood and a life taking care of my husband. But "life" still beckoned and I finally got to answer the call.

It was far from smooth sailing through the rough waters of cultural change. But I suppose that I was lucky enough to have a husband who went along with my competitive ambitions. And, looking back now, I should say it was a lot more than luck. Only a strong man would take me on. As long as it didn't diminish his ego or his role in the marriage, that is.

I guess I owe a lot to Betty Friedan. By the time women's liberation was a thing, my independent nature had been nurtured. I found other women who felt as I did and we began to meet to change the status quo. We started a consciousness raising conversation. Too bad I had to wait until 1970 to discover what that meant!

People often ask me, "How did you do it? How did you get here?" I wish I had some fantastic formula or a background in public service or in the Peace Corps. All I have is my own roadmap full of pot holes! And, I am not sure where "here" is, but I am glad I'm there!

Today, when I attend a gathering of women, either socially or professionally, I'm always awed. So much power in the room, so much sisterhood, so much shared information on so many levels. How do we harness that energy to advocate for support of the many complex issues facing women around the world today?

Several years ago the *New York Times Sunday Magazine* devoted its entire issue to the women it saw as icons who changed our world. Among the names and sleek professional photo portraits and beautiful, sophisticated writing were the women we expected to find: Elizabeth Taylor, Eleanor Roosevelt, Oprah Winfrey, Helen Keller, Coco Chanel, Jacqueline Kennedy, and Rosa Parks.

My icons are the women who, day after day, struggle as single moms, and in many cases hold down two jobs. Entrepreneurs, who live their dreams with so much faith in their vision they start their businesses with credit cards. Some women who have fled from violent and abusive relationships and have gone on to make productive lives for themselves and their families.

My icons are those women around the world who seek a better life for themselves and give a hand up to others who may not be as strong willed as some of us are. A hand up, not a hand out, as they say. Even if it's one woman at a time.

Recently my husband, Arnold, and I drove to Chicago to visit family. Ten years of my growing up during World War II were spent there. Important years that shaped my life for a long time into the future.

We lived around the corner from the rolling green Midway of the University of Chicago. Just a few blocks from the Field Museum where I spent so many hours as a young girl wandering the halls and storing away knowledge and memories. Today, you would never allow a young child to cross those wide, busy streets and enter the museum alone to wander those vast halls for fear of what might happen to her.

"Ally," my husband had said on that trip, "we have the car, let's go look at your old neighborhood." First reaction was, "Um, I don't think so. It may not be the way I remembered." Second reaction, "Well, maybe." And finally, "OK."

I remembered the exit on the Outer Drive and Lake Michigan and the rocks along the shore where my dad took me to walk and told me I would, at age eleven, have a new baby sister or brother. I remembered the street address, 5522 Cornell Ave, and the yellowish brick apartment building we lived in for those ten years. And the neighbors across the hall, whose *Life* magazine I grabbed every Friday afternoon. And the neighbor upstairs who always had a cigarette dripping in her hand and how she burnt one of the ivory keys on our new Baldwin piano. The piano my mother thought would turn me into a concert pianist.

The beautiful street was still a beautiful street and so was the building. The alley between the houses where I played kick-the-can with my friends and piled up newspapers we collected for the War Drive was still there. I felt good to see this.

"How about we go see your public school?" my husband next asked. Now he was on a roll! "OK," I said again, "It's right around the corner next to the big old Hotel Windermere." The school was there, but the Hotel Windermere, a gracious hotel with a large porch around the front, was long gone, replaced by a high-rise that faced Jackson Park.

But the school, Bret Harte, was so much smaller than I remembered. And it looked sad. Of course, it was just freshly built when I went there, so many years ago. Now it appeared to be aging, just like me.

Bret Harte Public School, Miss Gillian and her little bun on the back of her head. The school librarian who must have seen something in me at the tender age of eight. She piled my arms with all kinds of books that fed my imagination. Perhaps it was because my dad taught me to read the funny papers even before I went to school.

All in all, what a pleasant surprise that trip had been. Chicago and going back. Seeing where Dad's hosiery store had been on Monroe Street, now another high-rise. A bit sad to see, but the memories of those days behind the counter, learning the business, seeing a real Rosie the Riveter, are now committed to paper and are reconstructed to live again. There are parts of my life that going back, in my memory, are not so pleasant. And those memories as well have been committed to paper.

Through all those experiences—particularly Mama teaching me to be perfect and accomplished so I could marry a senator or doctor—the real me had been struggling to get out. In those days it was Alice the Good and Perfect, now I am some amalgam of yesterday and today, thanks to the two Bettys.

———

And that's why I have to look back…

Why I have to go back to so many places in the future. Because, you see, the past is my future. I wonder how I ever got through my life and came out on the other side of the tunnel intact and whole.

What makes a woman wise? I suppose I was stubborn, stronger than I thought, smarter than I gave myself credit for, and able to survive life's stumbling blocks. I also was prepared!

Was this really me? That girl in the 1950s who would skip college class to go trousseau shopping with my friend. Barbara and I planned engagement rings and wedding bands, wedding dresses, new apartments, furniture and linens. And of course we read the good girl bible—*Ten Steps to Be a Perfect Wife*. Only ten steps? "Lessons Learned over the Years that Make You a Survivor" would have been a better title.

Caught between the devil and the deep blue sea! Or, should I say, caught between Betty Crocker and Betty Friedan? I yearned to be me. Marriage is not for the frail of heart. Trying to be an independent women in the 1950s and 60s, not for the frail. Becoming a strong confident woman in your own right at any age, not for the frail.

I pushed on. Because of my love for anything connected to planes and flying, I started a newspaper at JFK Airport and then started the JFK International Chamber of Commerce. I loved my work.

My husband, Howard, worked for General Electric at the time. We were invited to a major social event with the brass. As a product of the 50s I dressed carefully and thought about the best way to support my husband and help push him forward. Forgot about me.

As we approached the dinner that night my husband turned to me and asked me not to discuss what I was doing at JFK. Just be a good girl and don't make waves! Apparently I looked the part of a woman who *did* know what she was doing and when the brass asked what I did, I told them!

A similar experience happened after that when I became Director of Marketing for the Metropolitan Transportation Authority in New York City. I was responsible for marketing five operating agencies and the JFK Express. The Executive Director of the MTA, my boss, turned to me as we were about to enter a meeting with the governors of New York and New Jersey for a presentation of my advertising campaign for The Train to the Plane, a combination of special train and bus to JFK International Airport.

"And you keep your mouth shut!" he yelled at me.

And that's why I have to go back—to see how far I have come from the restraints of the times that pushed me forward. I did it. I survived and came out as tempered steel.

Who but ourselves prepare us for marriage? Who but ourselves prepare us for the future?

Who prepares us for the stumbling blocks along the way?

How wondrous to have come out the other side of the tunnel and onto a new and better path!

What would my 1950s self think of me now?

Mr. and Mrs. Moses Rahmey
request the pleasure of your company
at the engagement of their daughter

Alice

to

Mr. Howard Borodkin
Sunday, the seventh of September
from seven until twelve o'clock
Duo-Art Academy
107-50 Queens Boulevard
Forest Hills, New York

R. s. v. p.

Alice's Engagement Announcement

2

Flaw in the Fairy Tale

Ellen, age 9 and Alice, just 20

Once upon a time, as all fairy tales begin, I lived in a big house with my mother, my father and my younger sister, Ellen. On the surface it all looked enchanting. Ellen, who was eleven years younger than I, had her own room down the hall from me. Her room was made to order for a little girl, all pink and white and feminine. The epitome of what Mama wanted us to be.

Yet, hard as I tried, I could never be perfect enough for Mama. My room, where I had to make my bed each morning, and hang up and pick up and clean up, before our housekeeper came to clean it, was never just right for my mother. Neither was I.

She had high expectations for me. Perfect, perfect, perfect. Piano, ballet, elocution lessons. My dad did as well, but showed it differently.

He was more thoughtful and tutored me in business and marketing, and read to me from Longfellow and Damon Runyon. When he would stop to interpret some of Longfellow's poems and I discovered how sad a poem was, I cried.

"Now look what you've done!" my mother would yell at him.

As far as he was concerned, he had the three most beautiful, talented women any man could hope to have. And he told us that all the time!

But I had to hand it to my mother. Between bouts of depression and drinking too much, she imparted a sense of who I was or rather who she thought I should be. Concerts, fine dining, beautiful clothes, for both of us. She was the Diva and I the Diva in Training! I believe, even though she didn't say it, that "Marry Well" was her motto.

Those days were some of the best times too. What memories! I loved dressing up. "Alice, go get dressed," Mama would call up the stairs. "And don't you dare get a spot on that dress!" she'd add as a final reminder that I needed to be perfect. Not just clean and presentable, mind you, but perfect.

And off we would go to shop and have lunch in the beautiful wood-paneled dining room of Chicago's Marshall Field Walnut Room. Every inch the Diva in her beautifully tailored gray suit or dress, her Stone Martin furs draped elegantly over her shoulder and her handmade "Hats by Ina" perched deliciously on her head.

But as soon as we came home it was back to my room for me. Just as I would run there after dinner and a full day of school, which I hated, and piano practice, which I also hated. But I loved that room. It was my sanctuary. No one, for whatever reason, disturbed me there. Even at thirteen—or maybe especially at thirteen—I needed this space, this peace where my dreams and imagination could flourish, where I could and did play out all my fantasies, listening to music now and forever connected to the war years of WW II.

As my sister Ellen grew older, however, she began to wander into my room. I adored Ellen and still do. But I'll never forget how she wreaked havoc with my dressing table and my favorite Madam Alexander dolls that my Dad bought for me on my birthday every year. Dolls who sat on the floor under the crisp white curtains. My children, as I thought of them. The ones I cared for as a mother for a child.

I had a few lipsticks on my dressing table. I now suspect that the little darling sister had crept into my room and had swiveled them open with the caps on! So much for the lipsticks! And my prized Madame Alexander doll in her green taffeta dress with black ribbons and lace lost her long blonde hair to my sister's scissors!

"Ellen!" I screamed, "How could you?" Her own doll-like face would scrunch up and the tears would flow. But I did love her so much that after I yelled at her, while my mother stood by laughing at her antics, which I did not think were funny at all, it was I who apologized as I wiped the tears away. I think it should have been the other way around!

My room also became a sanctuary for Ellen when she became ill. She would pad into my room and climb into bed with me to snuggle. Mumps, chicken pox, colds—during the worst of it, she would snuggle up as close as possible to me. I had never had anything and never did catch any of it! Until I turned thirty and had the measles, which sent me to the hospital with pneumonia, which in turn I proceeded to give to her and everyone else.

I loved that room! So many dreams, hopes, lessons learned. Too bad it was the only thing in that house without flaws.

Alice and Mama, 1946
Top of the Empire State Building
Hats and Gloves ruled the day!

3

Mama Was a Diva

Mama (L) and Mother-in-Law (R)

For a young girl about to enter her teenage years in the late 1940s, those nostalgic times were exciting and glamorous. The women wore hats that veiled their faces like softly hidden secrets. And gloves, always gloves, and long cigarette holders, and dresses, with huge shoulders, made of glamorous fluid fabrics that seemed to drift and float over their lithe bodies.

Mama was a DIVA! All the women, at least my mother's friends, seemed to be the most stylish I'd ever seen. Even Grandma Esther, my mother's mother, who lived in the Bronx in New York, was a diva in her own way. While she wore flowered print dresses and was a bit chubby, she carried herself with a certain air. Her gray curly hair was always in place, her makeup perfect and of course she smelled like Lily of the Valley.

I was never quite sure how much I should believe of all the stories she and Mama would tell about who they were and where they came from. And because of them who I was and how I should act. My sister Ellen and I seemed to have absorbed, like osmosis, a sense of who we were in the world, but both of us had a hard time accepting that fact.

You could easily spot the divas. What airs they had. Their beautiful clothes, bright red lipstick and matching nails enhanced their mannerisms and animated discussions of juicy family gossip. Perfect masks to hide the sorrow inside. The sorrow of an incomplete life, as I came to understand it later.

Although I didn't hear the word discipline, except when Mama had to speak to my school principal, which was often, I know that these women must have been disciplined in their daily routines. It seems I have inherited the discipline genes! My current daily morning routine of bath, makeup and hair, with clothes laid out on an already made bed, seems ingrained.

Hard to believe but, in the old days I was quiet and I thought I wasn't very bright, no matter what my teachers and parents told me, so I made people laugh and was well-behaved. Where did that get me? I followed my instincts, instead of the cultural rules of the day and as the saying goes, "Well-behaved women rarely make history."

Did I make history? I'm not sure about that, but I certainly made my own history!

Of course I had little to say about how my room would look back then. But that was all right because I liked my mother's taste. Good thing! When I was planning my wedding to the boy next door I came home one day to find a beautiful wedding dress on my bed! Mama had such good taste, and it never occurred to me that mothers shouldn't go out and buy their daughters' wedding dresses…I just thought her doing this showed she cared. *That* was important. But, as I think about it now, her purchase was just one more attempt to control my life.

Our house seemed filled with love and caring, along with the smell of good cooking and clean, fresh laundry. It was where flowers and plants lived a happy sunlit life, but where people had a more difficult time. This was a house that smelled of Mama's perfume. A house that sparkled and shone like Mama the Diva. A house very different from my friends' homes.

Mama was different too. She was beautiful, lively, funny, and she had a flair for life like no other mother I knew. I was so proud of her when she would come to my school…sweeping into the room leaving a scent of her perfume behind her.

But Mama was an actress acting out her perfect life and perfect image. Mama lived a life of fear and insecurity. Mama was a fraud.

The Diva, Mama (top left) in Hat (by Ina, 1946)
The pin Mama is wearing now is on a silver chain that I wear.

Dad, Mom, Grandma Esther, Grandpa Max, Aunt Jenny, Uncle Bernie
at Bill Miller's Riviera Supper Club, late 1940s

4

Victory Gardens and Trips on a Train

"The Most Famous Train in the World": The 20th Century Limited, an express passenger train on the NYC Railroad from 1902 to 1967

Growing up during the war we lived right across the street from the University of Chicago. I thought this was where the Coast Guard had set up headquarters, but it turned out it wasn't the Coast Guard at all. Truly it was the beginning of the atom bomb! Experiments were taking place that could have blown us all away—or so we thought! That first test actually was so weak it couldn't power more than a single light bulb.

That little experiment was called the first controlled, self-sustaining nuclear chain reaction...a key step in the Manhattan Project to develop the atomic bomb during World War II, engineered by scientist Enrico Fermi. I remember Mama and her diva friends discussing the possibility of the bomb later, after seeing a movie *The Beginning of the End*, which told the story of the development and the experiments at the university.

"Can you imagine?" Mama had said as she called out "Gin!" again. The rest of the divas just threw down their cards and began speaking about other subjects. After all, the aftermath of those tests, which were currently taking place, were very far away and had no bearing on how *their* lives might be changed. To a diva, life evolves around them. To hell with the outside world.

All our relatives lived back in New York. They already had felt the effects of the war. They knew about blackouts and they knew about submarines off the shore of Long Island. In Chicago, we were removed from the war, although we bought savings bonds, produced Victory Gardens and even, for a while, saved grease and round balls of aluminum foil.

Buying war bonds was a way to support the war efforts and every week my dad would give me money to fill a stamp book that would eventually purchase a bond. It was a big deal for each public school class to compete to see who would have the most stamp books collected.

Those Victory Gardens were my first and last venture into farming and gardening. Even today my deck and front lawn show off beautiful pots of already planted flowers purchased that way. New York high-rise style. Back then, adults and children alike had small plots of earth allotted to them in roped-off sections in parks and empty lots around Chicago. Here we could grow our own vegetables and send all the commercial fruits and veggies to our hero soldiers fighting for freedom. Victory gardens across the country ended up producing eight million tons of food!

My dad and I would buy vegetable seeds, radishes, lettuce and tomato plants. We'd line them up in neat rows that he would make and I would throw the seeds in. Being a city girl, I did not expect to find the creepy crawlers in the dug-up dirt. I left that chore to Dad.

One day as we went to check out our plot of ground, I saw a red piece of what I thought was paper and garbage. Then I discovered it was a radish.

"Daddy!" I called out, "Look what I found!" I can still hear him chuckling as he rushed over to look at "Our First Radish"!

"I told you we would have fresh vegetables," he laughed, causing me to smile. "Who knows? Maybe you will become a farmer." Now I realize, fat chance! I'm not happy with creepy crawlers of any sort! Hence the already planted pots!

Saving grease was for the production of soap. Mama got into the act by keeping an empty can of Maxwell House Coffee on top of the refrigerator that she dutifully poured fat into every chance she could. That was often—we used a lot of fat in those days. One day she decided to cook a goose. Don't know where she got that idea from, but you can imagine how much fat she poured into the can after that.

One day, from the kitchen, we all heard, "Oh my God, help me!" It seemed that Mama had poured the goose fat into the can, set the can on top of the fridge, gathered veggies from the fridge and then slammed the door shut. Perhaps the fat can had been perched too close to the edge, or perhaps she had slammed the fridge door too hard, who knows?

But down came the can filled to the brim with unsolidified fat, all over Mama, all over the pantry floor and out into the kitchen. Mama cried, Dad tried not to laugh and I remember just standing there. Just standing outside the kitchen watching the flood of fat flow all over the floor. After much arguing, crying and screaming, it was cleaned up.

I believe that was the end of saving fat for soap at our house.

Fat was plentiful back then, but silk, the material our stockings were made from, was mostly unavailable. It was being used instead for parachutes. We were stuck with rayon and soon nylon, which was just entering the picture. Do without our silk? The black market for hosiery quickly flourished and all the family in New York and Chicago, including my dad, took advantage of this not-so-legal means of obtaining precious silk.

I learned a lot about hosiery back then because the family was in the business. These were the pre-pantyhose days. Nylons during the war and for years after came with two separate legs and seams up the back. They were held up with girdles or garter belts. For some women, if you couldn't afford hosiery during the war, all you had to do was dye your legs a shade darker and paint a black line on the back of your legs to be the seams. I kid you not. And, there was a particular way to fold the stockings, if you had them. You needed to insert a piece of rounded-edge paper between the folds before storing them. That paper saw double-duty in our family. Since everyone seemed to be selling hosiery at that time, all letters were written from their stores and all used the hosiery paper as makeshift stationery.

Years later, I found a letter from my Aunt Lena, Dad's sister, written on that paper. Aunt Lena ran the family's New York hosiery and linen stores. Apparently Aunt Lena was the conduit for my dad and his black-market nylons.

February 18, 1941

Dear Moe (my dad),

Why don't you get nylons with the order you sent to me?
If you don't need nylons, anyone will take them off your hands
at a profit.

Maybe that's the reason your hosiery business fell down.
You must have what the people are asking for!

Well anyway, if you are losing money in your store, you
might as well come back to New York as you can make a
living here.

Kiss Allie and say hello to Ruthie.

During wartime, Mama—Ruthie—made it be known in no uncertain terms that she wanted to "go home" to New York to visit family. Never mind that travel was restricted to servicemen. Never mind that money was tight. Mama wanted to go home! And Daddy found a way. That's how it was!

How lucky I was to experience the thrill of one of the most famous and glamorous trains in history—the 20th Century Limited. It was so beautiful and exciting that they wrote a play and a movie about the train and the stories of the passengers. I had my own stories of those train trips, as you will see.

Mama and Daddy were from New York City—actually Mama was born there and Dad was born in Beirut, Lebanon but settled in New York when he was six. They met at age sixteen and stayed together for fifty tumultuous years. Their own "war years" as I came to understand later. *Their* war spilled over and engulfed all of us—perhaps more personally devastating than the real war.

My sister Ellen, being eleven years younger, does not remember all the arguments and even some nasty letters between our parents.

Mama, beautiful, neurotic, charming and insecure, was all about arguing and showing her anger. Dad was all about peace and quiet.

Many years later, after Mama died, Ellen and I began the chore of going through her things, cleaning out the closets and dresser drawers. In a shoe box pushed all the way back in a dark corner, I found a stack of letters between my mother, my dad and family members, written during the times we traveled to New York to visit the family. Circa 1941-1943.

I asked my sister if she wanted to read the letters, but she replied sharply, "Absolutely not!" What? I had thought they were interesting, they gave me a bit of insight into my parents' stormy love affair and marriage. My sister had different recollections.

The reason we were living in Chicago, while the rest of the family was back East, was because my dad was offered a lucrative job there. As the story goes, against all odds, Grandma Esther's wishes and Mama's tears, he packed up the family (Mama and me) and took us to live there. The rest of the family thought that we were going to live amidst cowboys and Indians, and likely would get killed by the Indians. I guess they never heard of Marshall Field's.

———

And so, war or no war, with family from both sides scattered between Brooklyn, the Bronx and Chicago, the trek back and forth by train was on.

How wonderful Chicago Union Station was for a ten year old. Bustling with energy, servicemen and servicewomen—actually little boys and girls playing soldier, I now think.

Announcements over the public address system would call out exotic names like Ohio, Tulsa and California. I can still smell the steam from the rail cars as it poured out as we followed the porter with our luggage to our berth. How romantic it seems now. It felt deadly and romantic at the same time, with such glamorous surroundings and people bustling all around and a world war going on—although I didn't give that part a second thought then.

Mama the Diva seemed to come right out of the movies. I remember those black and white films well. They featured beautiful women in their hats and veils and large padded shoulders, and of course gloves—and when I would look around me in the theater, all the women looked just the same. So sophisticated, I yearned to be one of them.

On that train, my mother was the epitome of those actresses as she breezily followed the porter. Our compartment with hidden berths and the cold smell of the train itself greeted us as the porter hefted our luggage over our heads to a shelf above. Those wonderful Pullman porters, so proud in their white starched jackets, winding their way through the cars with a tiny triangle playing a sweet sound announcing that dinner was served in the dining car. No one would think of going in for dinner without shirt and tie or hat and gloves.

I would change into a clean dress and high white stockings with black Mary Janes shining on my feet. My mother would make her entrance looking every inch the actress she was in her hat and veil, gloves and cigarette holder, leaving a trail of hyacinth perfume behind her.

The dining car was a picture of another time in my memory. The word gracious comes to mind. Little vases with real flowers, white tablecloths, a tiny yellow pencil to check off our selection for dinner on the menu.

I know now why all the boys in uniform vied for Mama's attention. Her reddish-blonde hair piled high under her hat and veil, her beautifully applied makeup and her knack for drawing attention. But she also did a bunch of playful but harmless flirting. It seemed she just needed to be the center of attention.

A quick stop in the club car after dinner, where glasses filled with martini's or scotch clinked, and a cloud of smoke enveloped everyone, and the music from the phonograph set up a false happiness… and then off to our compartment. The porter's soft knock on our door to see if we were ready for him to make up our berths came next.

Our tiny bathroom smelled of soap and cleanliness. The perfect place to scrub off the day's dirt as I prepared for bed. The feel of those white sheets and warm wool blanket gave me such a sense of peace that I happily drifted off to the sound of the clicking wheels on the track and the easy swaying of the train.

My mother would head to the club car, but came back every so often to check on me. She would smother me with kisses until I stirred to show her that I was fine. Her kisses smelled of vermouth and perfume. At last she would return for the night and climb into her berth under mine.

In the morning she would regale me with the stories from the club car the night before. On our way to breakfast, the little boy soldiers would say good morning and tip their hats to us and smile at my mother. Later she told me she had tipped the porter to keep an eye on me, too.

April 1942 (during one of our trips East)

Dear Moe,

Well, I'm back in New York. The patrols of planes go over the roof tops every 20 minutes and it drives me crazy. I get petrified with fear. I can't get used to it. Everyone here expects a real raid in return for the attack we gave them.

Everyone here thinks Allie and I look wonderful. And they think I look just beautiful. A little thin, but nice.

Met a charming man on the train. As good looking as a Greek god. We talked all night until 5 o'clock in the morning in the club car. He may come to see us in Chicago.

I love you and miss you. Truly all my love. Why do I always feel like I've let you down?

Ruthie

April 1942

Dear Ruthie,

I received your letter and all is well in Chicago. The store is doing fine and everyone here misses you. I will send you money next week.

Moe

April 1942

Dear Daddy,

I am writing to you from the club car on the train. We are going to eat soon.

I will be waiting for that date we made before I left. And don't forget to cover my dolls before you go to bed.

Love and XXXXXXX, Allie

Those trips back to New York City to hang out with the relatives were real eye-openers. Here we were, the Diva and the Diva in Training arriving with our luggage, going first to the Bronx and then on to exotic Brooklyn. First to Grandma Esther, my American-born grandmother, and the wild family of the Gottliebs.

I say wild because, when I was very young, I thought they were all friends of the family. I didn't know we were all related! Like all families they fought, they screamed at each other, they cried together, and then kissed and made up and did it over and over again.

Brooklyn, on the other hand, was home to my Grandma and Grandpa Rahmey. This was a Syrian Jewish community of close knit, clannish, let's-all-live-in-the-same-place relatives and continue our traditions from Damascus.

Mama was an outsider. She was considered to be "the blond" that Dad married "out of the community."

Later Mama would write to Dad from Brooklyn and the Bronx that all she wanted was to come home and the three of us to live in our little kingdom. No wonder I thought they were all wild! "Our kingdom" was quiet compared to theirs.

Tuesday, (no date) 1941

Dear Mosie,

When I get home leave a nice soft place on the floor, so I can fall flat on my face. I'm so tired of all the screaming and tears in the family. (This due to my uncles on both sides leaving for the army—but almost anything could get them riled.)

Do you miss us badly? You don't seem to. You seem to be having a nice vacation.

When I come home we are going to the movies. Just us. And just sit in our beautiful home and enjoy it.

All our love, Ruthie

Mama tried to create a kingdom, her own place in the world she created in her mind and in the real world as well. Everything, including family, "outside of our kingdom" hardly existed. Friends were made and dropped frequently, always with a whispered "Not our type." It was always done to preserve our "kingdom," our quiet, beautiful home.

Precious little I see now from Daddy to Mama. Funny I never noticed it before.

The Wild Family from the Bronx, 1950.
(L-R) Dad, Mama (seated in the back center), Alice, bottom right

5

On Being Perfect

Grandma Esther and Mama

L oving my mother was not an easy feat. And yes, there were times I know I didn't like her. Most young women go through that phase. But I never doubted for a minute that she loved me! When she and Dad came home from a night out, she would dash into my room and smother me with kisses that smelled of vermouth mixed with her hyacinth perfume.

Finally I would stir and sit up. "Now look what you did, Ruthie!" my dad would say. "Let the kid sleep."

Twice pneumonia struck me down, which she blamed on the harsh cold winters in Chicago. Mama would sleep with me and hold onto me as if her body and spirit would keep me from dying.

Yes, she had a difficult childhood. Her father died in China from TB when she was six months old. They never knew each other. Grandma went to work and Mama was shuttled from family to family until Grandma re-married.

This is where the stories of her background begin. She was told she was special and different. Her biological father was born in London, she was more cultured and educated than her half siblings born in the US, and she was always treated differently. Could it be this was when she developed into a diva?

I have a picture of her and my grandmother when Mama was about five or six. A pretty little blond girl sitting on her mother's lap. I search her eyes for clues to the beginnings of the insecurities and anxieties that molded her life and bedeviled her until she died at ninety-five.

More than being overly protective, Mama was possessive. I was never out of her sight. As a teen, I never went to camp nor was I permitted to attend a sleepover at a girlfriend's house. But I did go to the finest supper clubs in Chicago and New York, saw every play and show on Broadway, attended concerts, and traveled with my parents wherever they went.

That possessiveness carried through into my marriage. She needed to be with me every day, almost not allowing me to forge relationships with other young women and their babies. If Dad had not stopped her, later she would have invaded my weekends with my husband!

I remember my dad saying to her, "Ruthie, love is like quick silver. If you squeeze it, it slips through your fingers. But hold it loosely and it will stay in the palm of your hand."

There was always competition between my in-laws and Mama that became worse as time went on. Whose house would we choose for holiday dinners? How often did I go to my mother-in-law's house? "Please come for dinner more often" was a constant plea.

Later, that competition turned into any and all dinners, holiday or not, being at my house. I loved to cook, and because of Mama's training, everything was "perfect."

"I always said Alice could do it all," she would brag to everyone.

The brandy she had grown so attached to helped her to make up stories about who she was, where she came from and what made her so special and different. We heard those tales a million times and still don't know how much is true about her life.

When I was young, our financial situation was good and so life was pretty good as well. But for Mama, it always seemed as if that little black cloud of fear and anxiety hovered over her and started to rain if she thought she might be in danger of losing everything.

Mama was beautiful, funny, alive and creative. I think she knew it by the way she looked on the outside, but I'm not so sure now that she truly believed it on the inside.

One never knows what goes on in a marriage or a home—or a person's mind. She was a great actress! Years later, as development director at a safe house, I watched from a window as a woman in her nightgown and mink coat stepped out of a cab in her slippers. Her hair was disheveled and one eye was bruised. Suddenly, Mama flashed before me. Beautiful, but battered in a different way.

Her way of hiding was twofold: there was her brandy glass...and her penchant for perfection. Not just for her but for my father and me and later for my sister. And definitely for our home.

I always considered myself fortunate to live in such a beautiful home. Chinese antiques, beautiful, tasteful furnishings and lots of plants. Her cooking, and she was a great cook, filled the air with delicate aromas. It was all a part of the picture Mama painted for herself.

Yet, almost anything could trigger one of the screaming and yelling scenes. A bed not perfectly made, clothes lying out, a bug walking on the window sill. Her unhappiness with something any of us might have said or inadvertently done.

Was it the brandy speaking? Was it her insecurity and anxiety? Was it the times? Where *did* all that anger come from?

———

Mama was beautiful. Until she reached her sixty-fifth birthday, that is. First she had a stroke that impaired her speech and caused a slight paralysis of her right side. But the brain went on. Dad and I picked her up from the hospital and took her home.

But not before she stopped to let loose on a young doctor. "You son of a bitch!" she yelled, her good hand and finger pointed in his face, "Never, ever speak down to me again!" Well, her speech had sure returned.

She got better and began to look like herself again, dressing in the role she had invented for herself over the years. Beautiful! Smart! Funny! Mama.

But the depression returned, and with it the brandy and the pills. The doctor recommended shock treatments. My mother, having shock treatments. It was downhill all the way after that.

But still she would attempt to "put her face on" as she said, and would pull out her clothes and jewelry. Especially her pearl necklace that she prized above all. After she died we found out the prize was a genuine imitation.

We watched as she slid further away from us, into her make-believe world. Her makeup began to look clownish and her clothes, though still fashionable, began to look tired. We all began to look tired.

Therapy was out of the question. The snap-out-of-it attitude prevailed in those days. I always imagined that if she'd had therapy she would have been a powerful force to deal with. I recognize now how smart and business-savvy she was, even on her worst days.

In my mind I will always see her sweeping into a room looking beautiful, smelling wonderful, and making everyone laugh at some silly joke.

I also recognize now that she left me some of those wonderful qualities and for that I am grateful.

My father was always "Daddy" to me. In fact, as an adult, I had his phone number listed under Daddy. And he will forever be Daddy to me.

As the story goes, when Grandma Esther, my mother's mother, first met Daddy she collapsed from his exotic dark good looks. Black hair slicked back, dark brown olive-colored eyes, passionate about life. No wonder. Like everyone else, no one ever thought there was such a thing as a Jewish Arab! Mama was blond and thin. A contrast in cultures that became the fabric of my life and made me who I am today.

Small in stature, Dad made up for it with his bouncy walk and personality. Mama called him Little Caesar. But along with his energetic personality came his migraines. Too much stress, I always thought, trying to make Mama happy, making both sides of the family happy.

And then there was me. Alice the Good and Perfect! Always, as my Aunt Mally would say, "So pretty and round." No wonder I grew up always thinking I was fat. I inherited the big brown eyes, long lashes of my Middle Eastern grandmother and my aunts, and also the round, full figure that made them look like Italian opera stars.

Mama used to say I was my father's child and that she just happened to be there when I was born. It always delighted me to hear that. But secretly I always thought I was like her and it scared the hell out of me. Her moods, up and depressive, her temper, her striving for perfection, and her fear of never having any money and security. And, worst of all, her feeling of superiority over everyone else.

It took many years for me to forgive her for those traits, as understanding of her insecurity didn't come until so much later in my life.

After speaking to my sister over the years, I realize now that she took the brunt of Mama's downhill behavior after I married and left the house. No wonder she didn't want to read the letters!

And yes. Some of that depression was passed on to me, and I struggled through it all. But it turns out I was and am stronger than she was, and like my dad, always striving for the next thing in my life.

Dad at 17 or 18 (Mama called him her Rudolph Valentino)

6

Rosie the Riveter

1942 Poster "We Can Do It!" by J. Howard Miller

During the war, while we were still living in Chicago, I went to work with Daddy and learned to sell and order hosiery and lingerie, stock shelves, balance the register and take inventory at his hosiery business, working there on weekends. I was eight or nine when I started. Dad gave me a lot of responsibility, and if I made a mistake, it was chalked up to "a learning experience."

One learning experience of a different sort was unforgettable. Not too long after I'd been working there a saleswoman and I were held up while Dad went out to get us lunch. It might not have been such a big deal—no one got hurt—but it made the front page of the Chicago daily newspaper. There we were, me posing, hiding behind tall cartons filled with merchandise, peeking out at the robber. Back then it was common for city newspapers to cover local stories in depth. I don't recall why or when the reporter showed up with his camera. The important thing was that, in the photo, my long brown curls hung prettily over my white blouse and my beautiful brown plaid skirt was spread out daintily around me. Shades of Mama the Diva? My dad was proud of me, but I think more proud of the picture—he sent it to his mother in New York, who framed it and put it in the living room for all to see! I now have that copy of the newspaper story in my office.

Gunman Frightens Girl, 7, in Holdup of Dad's Store

Proud She Didn't Cry, Child Tells Police

Alice Rahmey, 7, was pretty frightened today when a man with a gun entered the hosiery shop of her daddy, Moses Rahmey, at 5523 Cornell av. and ordered her into the back room.

But, she proudly told police later, she didn't cry. She just went along with the store manager, Miss Harriet Siegan, 24, who also was under instructions from the gunman.

Alice mustered courage to peek from behind some packing cases as the robber pocketed $35 from the cash register and fled. Then she told Miss Siegan the man was gone—and Miss Siegan called Central police.

Seven-year-old Alice Rahmey, safe behind packing boxes, just couldn't resist a peek to see if store bandits had gone. (Herald-American photo.)

Just as memorable, Dad's store was also where I got my first glimpse of Rosie the Riveter. I watched wide-eyed as these women would come directly to the store from their shifts at the steel mills. Since the draft was sucking up all the men into the armed forces, women during the war took physically demanding jobs in defense factories, shipyards, steel mills, lumber yards and munitions plants. It was their civic duty. One of the national slogans during that time was, "The more women at work, the sooner we win." And, for many, it was probably the first time in their lives they were so independent, earning money for physical labor. Most of us have seen the World War II picture of Rosie, with her long eyelashes, fresh bright red lipstick, clean fingernails—and bulging biceps. Pretty good image, but that picture left out the rough red hands and greasy clothes and worn tired look on the faces of all the Rosies who took over for the men who went to war.

My eyes would widen further when a woman, who you could tell was a Rosie, came into the store and opened her purse. You could see the money from her newly cashed paycheck rolling out to the waiting hands of the clerk to pay for her feminine lingerie and her silk stockings with the seams up the back. Grease and dirt suddenly disappeared as she fingered the fine black-market silk items.

It wasn't until years had passed that I realized that Rosie the Riveter meant so much more. For me the poster of Rosie, and the slogan underneath, "We can do it!" was and is the epitome of what women are capable of. Norman Rockwell in his *Saturday Evening Post* cover for May 29, 1943 portrayed her as the female Paul Bunyan, stronger than we could imagine for a woman. A copy of that poster decks my office wall to remind me.

I have a feeling that many of these women found it difficult to go back to their earlier lives after the war, now that they had tasted the freedom and independence and the pay check at the end of the week. Perhaps this was the beginning of feminism. It took a war.

Looking back, I realize now that the culture of the late 1940s and 50s was stifling for so many young women, Rosie the Riveter aside. At times I think it was bordering on puritanical. How times have changed. I still cannot believe that with raging hormones we didn't go any further then heavy petting! A little different today as we battle teenage pregnancies and lectures about safe-sex practices and "no means no."

Of course there were rumors in high school in my day about those "bad girls" who "put out." I can recall only one of "those girls." She told me the facts of life while sitting on a curb watching the boys play kick-the-can. I vividly recall her words.

Listening to her, I matched what she told me with what my dad had told me one day in a B&G Restaurant when I asked him about sex or babies or something. He'd drawn pictures on a paper napkin about flowers and pollen and other "stuff." OK, I got it!

But always in the back of my mind I needed to be Alice the Good and Perfect. And I was…to a point. I suppose my reticence with boys was all part of the training to "marry well." That meant remain a virgin. Be beautiful. Be classy. Be perfect. Trained in classical music, ballet, the arts—the fine-tuning needed if you wanted to marry a man with a future. As in, "he's a doctor, or he's a politician, or he's a lawyer." Oh, I had been trained well!

No one ever thought to ask the young lady what she wanted to be or do. And we never thought to speak up either. Who thought we could run for office, become a lawyer, a writer or, for heavens sake, a pilot? That was not on our radar screen.

Truth be told, Rosie the Riveter was an anomaly to us. Awe-inspiring, yes, but still more like a caricature than a real person. Larger than life. A part of wartime.

After the war, for so many of us, it continued to be all about marriage, children (pre-birth control pill), perfect home. Wonderful cook, excellent hostess. Support the man and his career. But the seeds of dissatisfaction had been sown.

7

My Cocoon

Alice, Graduation from P.S. 144

When I was thirteen, we moved from Chicago to Forest Hills, an affluent neighborhood in the borough of Queens, New York. World War II was just over. I had mad crushes on the boys in my class. In fact, just about any boy who looked at me. But disaster courted me with each boy friend. I was always in love, and spent many hours crying about "lost love" to my father.

Dad would hear me crying, knock softly on my door, step into my sanctuary to sit on the edge of my bed to sooth me and tell me stories or read to me from one of our favorite books. I loved his stories. Especially as he would wipe away my girlish tears and pat my head. I am not sure how embellished his stories were, but who cared? He was a great storyteller.

One of his favorite stories was about the time during World War I when he got arrested. It seemed he'd been a bit of a hellion when he was a kid. He and some friends had jumped the fence of a New York rail yard to hang out around the trains. The cops arrested him and called his parents. Although all the other kids got bailed out by their folks, Dad's mother left him there overnight to stew a bit and learn a lesson. As Dad tells the story, when he got out, Grandma Rahmey, his mom, pinched his ears all the way home.

Once I settled down after one of his good bedtime stories, tears all dried, he would go back to Mama, who was waiting to hear the details of my sadness. I wonder now why she didn't come to me.

That bedroom in Forest Hills had been a wonderful haven. I look back now and realize that it was a cocoon from which I emerged as a slightly damaged butterfly. My beautiful room of blue and yellow flowered wallpaper. Maple furniture lined the walls and in one corner was a kidney-shaped dressing table with a white organdy skirt. Fledgling makeup sat on a mirrored tray along with my very first bottle of toilet water—Lily of the Valley.

Next to my bed was a maple night table with a "genuine imitation" antique lamp that resembled the old candle and wick-style lamps of a past time. It had beautiful painted red flowers on the top and bottom globe. But inside, of course, was an electric bulb. Next to the lamp, which was standing on a perfectly ironed, hand embroidered doily my mother had sewn, was a radio and a box of tissues.

Tucked into a corner next to my dressing table was what was called a ladies chair. It was a small delicately tufted chair of blue and yellow and white flowers to match my wallpaper. I loved that chair! I suppose because it lent an aura of completing my room and giving me another special place to read and dream.

I spent a lot of time gazing out the windows at the boy next door. I remember the windows overlooked a big crabapple tree that stood close by in our neighbor's back yard. That apple tree had apples that would drop all around creating a sort of apple sauce for the squirrels. My mother was sure the squirrels were drunk on fermented apples! They would scamper up the back stairs and try to enter the back door.

Little did I suspect that those neighbors would become my in-laws.

In our family, dinner was served every night in the dining room. Contrary to today's constant communication, we were not allowed to answer the phone during dinner. I couldn't wait until dinner was over so I could retreat to my room where I had a telephone extension and could speak to my friends in private. But briefly. A voice from the stairwell, either my mother or father, would yell up, "Not too long, Allie!"

After dinner there was one more chore. Although we had sleep-in help, I had to clear the table and dry the dishes before disappearing for the night.

At last I could retreat to my room. I would shut the door behind me, turn on the lamp and the radio and head for my dressing table to peer at my reflection in the flowered framed mirror. Ugh! I hated my thick eyebrows. And my nose was way too big. I fiddled with the makeup.

Radio in those days was the creation of imagination. Music flowed from that little brown box and I would dream the dreams of a thirteen year old.

Were we rich? While growing up I always thought Dad had a lot of money. The house in Forest Hills was large and beautiful and, as

Mama would point out, had forty-four windows that had to be kept shining all the time. The good thing was that Mama made us help in the dinner preparation and table setting.

But Mama the Diva had visions of grandeur, I now see. And Dad, adoring Mama, was always ready to please her and spoil her. We had a gardener who came once a week, a laundress once a week, and sleep-in help. Having that help was not unusual after the war years and in Forest Hills.

Yes, Dad had money made during World War II from his hosiery and lingerie shops and other stores he had opened in other states right after the war, places where he had contacts who told him where opportunity might be to become successful. But now I see that the money came in one hand and out the other. No investments. Just a lot of spending. I think he enjoyed being able to do the things that made him and everyone else happy...

Grandma Esther, my mother's mother? She had always had a bad ankle that never healed right after some sort of accident. Off to Columbia Presbyterian Hospital, the best surgeon he could find, and it was fixed.

Grandma Rahmey, Dad's mother? She needed cataract surgery, so Dad sent for a doctor who was visiting from South America who he knew had perfected cataract surgery. I always wondered if Dad blamed himself for her death as she died on the operating table.

Daddy's favorite day was to take the four of us to the fur district in Manhattan and buy us all fur coats, followed by dinner in the Waldorf Astoria Starlight room.

When I grow up, I remember thinking back then, I will waltz and dance like Rita Hayworth in a pink and black lace gown. Today the glamour of the 50s still appeals to me and someday I am going to buy myself a black and pink lace dress to float around in.

The reality of those evenings, though, as I went about my imagining, was homework, and preparing my clothes and school books for the next day. I had a large walk-in closet, almost like a hideaway when I needed it. I remember needing it often.

You never knew when Mama would fly off the handle. I now recognize she was a bit spoiled. Daddy was not so calm either. But he tried hard to please my mother and keep peace in the house. When things got out of hand, as I saw it, I would retreat to my closet and shut the door.

So my room became a haven of sorts and every night I had my routine. I spent hours reading Nancy Drew, a young and innocent detective, and Cherry Ames, Registered Nurse. Not to leave out *Life* magazine and, although I was just thirteen, *Seventeen* magazine.

Overall, our house was perfect. Mama wouldn't have it any other way! It was a magical place to look at. Bright with sunshine and plants and flowers. Along with my bedroom, everything was furnished in good taste, with striped satin wallpaper in the dining room and the ever-present yellow flowered wallpaper in the spotless kitchen. This house was great for flowers and plants.

At times not so great for humans.

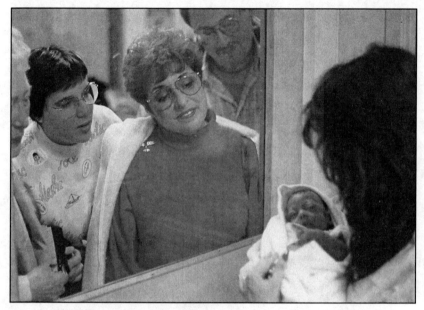

Generations: (L-R) Mina Borodkin, Julie, Alice, Howard.
Our first look at our Grandson Zac, 3lbs!

8

Diva in Training

No caption necessary!

What was so wrong with a good girl-please Mama upbringing, anyway? Life was simpler. As I look back, life in Chicago and then in New York when I was a teen was focused only on the next date or school test or Mama telling me, "Go practice the piano!" as she came out of the kitchen wiping her hands on a kitchen towel. Yes, I was a Diva in Training! Even at age 15. The Betty Crocker Syndrome was alive and well at our house. Ballet lessons, piano lessons, cooking lessons from the Diva, concerts, museums, all with the unspoken intent of marrying well.

And each time I had a date was a moment in time. I was always falling in love.

My first encounter with puppy love was in 1948, with the life guard at Brown's Hotel in the Catskills. And it was also my first sighting of Jerry Lewis! I never saw my dad laugh so much and so hard as when Jerry Lewis took the stage or ran around the lobby and the pool like a loony bird. These were high times for us.

And oh, the food! Couldn't make up your mind what you wanted to eat? No problem. The waiter brought one of everything on the menu for you to taste, eat or whatever. So it shouldn't be a total loss, he brought a bit of his opinions as well. Just make sure his thumb wasn't in the soup!

Such a deal. A weekend of everything you could ask for from swimming to skating at the indoor ice skating rink. People-watching in the lobby...*Did you see what she was wearing?*

The clothes! Pulling into the driveway you could watch the bell boys unloading the cars and hanging the wardrobes of sparkling evening gowns, bathing suits, golf clothes, jeweled sweaters, and men's elegant suits and sports jackets on the rolling hangers. Most of us were only there for three days...*but let's bring the mink stole anyway, and don't forget your gloves!*

Not a pair of flip-flops to be seen! Not one baseball cap on backward.

But seriously, all I thought about was boys. I was mesmerized by Paul, my first young man. Handsome, bright, with large horn-rimmed glasses. A college man, not a boy, for heavens sake. I was still in high school; dating a college man was something to flaunt to all my so-called girl friends. Dating a handsome college man was even better. Discussing where you wanted to go to college and flaunting good grades were not nearly as important as flaunting an engagement ring and getting married.

Part of being a Diva was my Boy Education. I learned a lot about what boys liked as I began dating. Paul loved wrestling, not with me until later, but real wrestling with sweaty bodies, in a ring surrounded by cigar-smoking men and people yelling, "Slay the guy!" or something like that.

Perhaps coffee and cake afterward and then a bit of necking on the sun porch couch. Without fail, just as Paul would settle in and the serious smooching would begin, a voice from the top of the stairs would call out, "Allie, please bring me a glass of water."

So dutiful daughter of the 1950s, who had forgotten we had two bathrooms where Dad could get his glass of water, would trudge up the stairs with glass in hand to hear whispered, "Get him out soon, please." So that was that and Paul left.

How in heaven's name were we able to control our hormones in those days and not go further? Easy. I knew my parents would kill me if I did. And so it went.

———

A moment in time. My next love, Mike, another college man. A member of the biggest fraternity on campus. Was I dreaming? He asked me out! Mike liked boxing instead of wrestling. Such diversity in my education! His uncle was a famous referee. I heard later that Mike had become a sports writer.

One time Mike insisted I call him when I got home from school to confirm our Saturday night date. No cell phones, blackberries, blueberries, I-pads. Just plain old black phones with a dial.

"Oh, my God," I thought, "What if his mother picks up the phone? I'll hang up!" Remember, this was 1950 after all, some of us were in Betty Crocker mode! Who called boys?

As usual, after the date Mike and I would settle in on the sun porch sofa and another moment in time reared its head again. "Allie, would you please bring me a glass of water?" muttered from the top of the stairs.

Glass of water, followed by, "Get him out soon, please." A stage whisper that the neighbors down the block could hear.

There were many more moments in time and other loves all accompanied by the glass of water routine.

…Until the real moment in time when Howard the Boy Next Door slipped a ring on my finger and asked, "Marry me?" I said yes and I did and that was a real moment in time.

However, that didn't stop the "Allie, may I have a drink of water?" routine. It just changed. Parked in Howard's car in front of my house, steamy windows and all, I would hear the front window of my parents' bedroom open and then, "Alice, why don't you and Howard come inside instead of necking in the car?" The whole neighborhood heard that one, I'm sure.

9

The Bettys

Every Young Girl's Dream: My Wedding, 1951

In the New York City of the 1950s we girls/women had one thing on our minds: marriage. We were living the dream the women's magazines and Betty Crocker said we should not only appreciate but happily embrace.

I made no lists of what I was looking for in a mate, as my young friend Melody told me she had made before she married. Interestingly, she also had decided not to have children. Who thought about those decisions in the 1950s? We just got married! We had children, it was expected!

I never thought about a list. And I had no plans for the future after the wedding day. No options either. I graduated college on Thursday and got married that Sunday!

Yes, I married the boy next door! Back then it was the most romantic story and was the proper thing to do! His parents, not doctors or lawyers but close enough, were both classical musicians and composers—his father a cellist, his mother a pianist. Yet it seemed my father-in-law was always trying hard to keep up financially.

I followed *The Good Wife Book* (the precursor to the *Good Wife Guide: 19 Rules for Keeping a Husband Happy,* for sale on Amazon). I didn't realize it at the time, but I was following a script written by my grandmothers, my mother and probably some very uninformed men.

And then Betty Friedan came out with *The Feminine Mystique.*

And, with the publication of that book, the ground shook. I was now feeling pulled in two different directions, Betty Crocker pulling one way and Betty Friedan, the other. Betty C's recipes and smiling goodness, and Betty F's harsher look at life, which some were calling a manifesto. The one: how to be the perfect wife (at least in the kitchen). The other: Dare to pursue your own dreams! Don't live through your children and your housewifely duties! The beginning of women's lib.

Betty Crocker:

Every morning before breakfast, comb hair, apply makeup and a dash of cologne. Does wonders for your morale and your family's too! Think pleasant thoughts while working and a chore will become a 'labor of love.' Have a hobby. Garden, paint pictures, look through magazines for home planning ideas, read a good book or attend club meetings. Be interested—and you'll

always be interesting! If you have a spare moment, sit down, close your eyes and just relax.
—from *Betty Crocker's New Picture Cook Book, 1961*

Betty Friedan:

Millions of American women stand victim of 'the feminine mystique,' a philosophy that has convinced them that their only commitment is the fulfillment of a femininity found in 'sexual passivity, male domination and nurturing maternal love.' They are dangerous in that, unable to find their real selves, they feed emotionally on their children—thus crippling them—and are unable to satisfy their husbands because they cannot enjoy sex for sex's sake. They try to relieve their feelings of depression and emptiness by seeking 'strained glamor.' They have won the battle for suffrage but little else.

This is the damning indictment levelled by Betty Friedan in her highly readable, provocative book.

– The New York Times, 1963

And I? Cooking, kids, house, pleasing everyone but me. Rumblings of wanting more. To be validated for the whole person. It was an itch I was longing to scratch.

10

Genes and Myths

The Rahmey Hosiery and Lingerie store in Harlem, 1920

Well, Betty Friedan may have been the catalyst to letting loose all the itches, but she couldn't override my Betty Crocker side completely. Nor could she do anything about my genes. By the time I was ten, it was pretty much certain I'd make someone a good wife. That was in the genes...and Mama made sure of it. But even she doesn't get all the credit, I had some very interesting family members, not to mention the relatives I inherited by marriage.

If Mama was a superior housewife, Daddy was the quintessential breadwinner and entrepreneur, and I thank him for those genes.

When I was about sixteen, Dad opened a store in Harlem called Rahmey Hosiery and Lingerie. It struck a chord with many retailers on 125th Street, who asked if he was related to the Rahmeys that had the linen store in the 1920s. That was Grandpa Rahmey and his brother. And so it goes!

I worked in Dad's store, as I had done in Chicago, and it was there I learned about responsibility among other things. We lived in a nice neighborhood in Forest Hills, Queens at the time. Far from the streets of Harlem.

One Saturday morning—I was about sixteen, I recall—running down the steps into the kitchen, I plopped myself down and poured myself a cup of coffee. Dad, reading *The New York Times*, put the paper down, looked at me and said, "What are you doing?"

I replied like the ultimate New York brat, "Waiting for you to drive us to the store."

"Really?" he asked. "Well, I'm the boss and I'll leave when I'm ready. You leave now and take the subway, open up the store, count the cash, make sure the inventory is clean, and I'll see you later."

Being Alice the Good at that time, I did exactly that. On the way out the door he yelled, "And don't make any dates until after you close up at 6:30!" So much for dating on Saturday night!

———

The small neighborhoods of New York City felt like home to me. And, still today, when I walk into a Middle Eastern restaurant amidst the smell of rice, simmering tomatoes, cumin, allspice, olive oil, and other spicy delights, I am assaulted with memories.

There before my eyes I conjure up Grandma Rahmey. Dad's mother, born in Damascus during the late 1800s, the product of a society where men ruled. Or so they thought!

The men paid the bills, shouted at the kids—there was always a houseful of cousins—played backgammon on those intricately carved inlaid tables straight from Damascus, and did the grocery shopping. Surely no woman could possibly fathom the intricate art of shopping for groceries and negotiating prices. Let alone pick the finest fruits and vegetables.

The unusual thing I learned later was that these same women were always involved in the stores and businesses that the men owned! Why am I surprised?

Today the third and fourth generation of Syrian Jews are college educated—doctors, lawyers…and many are in the finance industry. Thanks to my sister Ellen, who still lives right in the middle of the community in New York, I receive all the magazines and gossip every week or so at my home in Denver. Doesn't take me long to recognize a Rahmey when I see a picture of one. They still are dark, handsome and look like my dad and all my cousins.

If you are in New York and visit lower 5th Avenue in Manhattan, you will still see the names of those who originally opened those import-export houses. Names like Haddad, Sutton, Bibi, and Hannan in gold on store fronts or office buildings. My dad among them. Offices of Moses Rahmey, on a brass plaque that was, until just a few years ago, on a building on 5th Avenue and 23rd Street.

Grandma Rahmey, slight of build, as long as I knew her, flashing large brown eyes, busy strong hands and always the gold bangle bracelets from her native Damascus clanking musically on her arms. Now I wear mine and hers, clinking away as I move about.

But oh, we all knew her well! When we'd all get together, her humming would remind us that she was listening intently to every word and sound her family was making. Dad and Grandpa Eli would sit discussing business in Arabic and French in the large family dining room over small cups of Arabic coffee while Grandma would hum and stir those aromatic pots in the nearby kitchen…and listen.

I, as usual, sat next to my dad and listened carefully too, trying to pick up a few words here and there. Business training and language education all rolled into one. Their conversation always led to raised voices that prompted Grandma to stop humming and add her two cents to the conversation.

"Moses! Eli!" she would shout, and go off in a torrent of Arabic that was way over my head to get even one word of it.

My grandparents' wedding picture, taken in Damascus, now hangs in my office. There's Grandpa Rahmey wearing his fez at a jaunty angle, and Grandma in her long white dress, dark hair piled high under her veil, cinched waist and full bosom. They both look stunned! But if you look closely you will see their fingers barely touching. (See photo, page 68.)

She may have looked stunned in the wedding picture, but the three pictures below the wedding picture, taken in later years, show remarkable strength as the family grew in Damascus, Beirut and finally America.

Questions always come as I stare at those old photos. Did they love each other? Was it an arranged marriage? Did they learn over the next fifty years or so to love and share, in happiness and health, and sad moments in a new country, America?

I never thought about the women in my life until it was too late to ask. When I was eighteen, suddenly both Grandma Esther and Grandma Sophia Rahmey passed away within six weeks of each other. Only sixty-five years old, but at my age they looked old to me. I not only didn't ask, but at eighteen I didn't know what to ask.

Now I have questions. Who are you? Where did you come from? Tell me your story. Now I think of them often and remember some stories I heard about their lives…

Friday nights in Grandma Esther's house in the Bronx, with aunts, uncles, cousins, in-laws and out-laws. Everyone in those days lived in the same building or just around the corner. Sharing one phone, arguing, loving, a culture long gone.

Constantly gossiping, spilling and spinning tales that may or may not have been true. Was my gorgeous blue-eyed blond cousin Leonard really illegitimate from an affair one of my uncles had, but raised by my aunt, his wife, as her own?

Was Uncle Julie's tale of World War I and how he was wounded after the Armistice by one of his buddy's accidentally discharged gun true? Or, perhaps he limped due to arthritis? But to me those stories and subtle intrigues became part of the fabric of my own story…the stuff soap operas are made of!

Grandma Esther died on a Friday night sitting around the Shabbat dinner table with her family all around her. Coming back from the funeral on Sunday, we ate the massive amounts of food she had prepared for that Friday night dinner.

I slipped into her bedroom to smell her face powder now puddling with my tears and slipped her compact into my pocket. I have it still, but the aroma of her perfume and powder lingers only in my mind now.

———

I don't have all the answers about my grandparents, but I know without a doubt where I got my love of cooking. Both grandmas cooked enough to feed the homeless and sometimes, given the fact that I did not recognize some of my "cousins," perhaps they did!

At thirteen, every Sunday I served Turkish coffee on big brass trays in Grandma Rahmey's house in Brooklyn's enclave of Syrian Jews. There always were myriads of invited guests and anyone else who, as the saying goes, "Come over sometime!" and so they did. All dressed up as well. This after the intrigue of all those Friday evenings in the Bronx. More soap opera stories followed, with hot topics like how and why this one married that one and how they came from Damascus and Beirut together clinging to each other for support.

Again, listening to family stories, this time in Arabic and English. Talk of business and the stores they owned. More gossip about relatives and neighbors. Grandma Rahmey giving instructions and orders, from how to bring up your kids, run your life and your business, to sharing her recipes.

All my dear aunts that I adored following suit. Everyone speaking at the same time. I understand now where I got my training in interrupting, and speaking loudly in order to be heard over that raucous bunch!

I am overwhelmed at both the grandmas' fortitude to move on and through life. To create their lives from the ashes and hardships they must have endured. No Social Security, no pensions and no food stamps, no health insurance, no counselors to ask for help. Just their strength and willpower and each other. Family that fought, cried and lived their lives together.

One grandma coming to a new world, the other born in America, but both no strangers to adversity.

Grandma Rahmey...dark hair, dark intense eyes that saw everything, strong hands that had learned how to make hats in Damascus, speaking French mixed with Arabic and English. Myth? Truth? Did the story grow larger over time?

I will always associate wax fruit in a cut glass bowl—price labels still on—with her, along with all the aromas I try to recreate in my kitchen. Now I know why some of the items I've bought over the years still have their price tags on them months and sometimes years later.

To me, she will always be remembered for her humming, followed by whatever she shouted in Arabic that quieted the loud voices of the men. I also remember she was always singing, especially to drown out the conversations that were not to her liking.

And then there was Grandma Esther…I remember her the way I knew her, with gray curly hair that she would ask me to trim for her. She sure trusted me. I was only thirteen! But the picture of her and my mother at five or six years old showed a grandma I didn't know. Mama was wearing a locket I now have tucked away. The locket bears Mama's teeth marks.

The "Gibson girl" in the photo in white shirtwaist and belted tiny waist, her dark curly hair piled on top of her head, all topped by a voluptuous bosom! That grandma was a looker! So I am blessed with the curly hair and a bosom. Seems like I'm the one that inherited all the bosoms from both sides of the family!

Now I look at Mama's picture closely to see if she was as fragile as family told me she was. Those eyes. Was the beginning of the insecurities that molded her life and bedeviled her until she died at ninety-five hiding in those eyes? Did I inherit those dark clouds of depression from her?

And there is something, I see now, about Grandma's face that shows a small smile hiding a strong jaw and sad eyes, along with a "Don't start with me!" look. Now I know where that look, which people tell me I have from time to time, came from.

Both grandmas, I am told, were determined once they made up their minds to do something, they did it. They stuck to their values and ideals and set out to prove that life is what you make it. I'm sure I see a bit of me in those virtues.

The two grandmas could not have been more different as were the worlds they came from. One brought up in a male dominated society in the Middle East in a traditional Orthodox Jewish family. The other born in America, but I never asked about where she came from and why was she so angry at her brothers and sisters all the time? Now, no one to ask. Who were their mothers? Where *did* they come from?

Why was my mother brought up by grandparents from England? It's really sketchy. Who were they? As a young bride with a six-month-old child, Grandma Esther was already a widow. Her husband, my biological grandfather, died in China from TB during the Boxer Rebellion. He was an exporter of Chinese antiques. So Mama went to stay with his parents as Grandma Esther sought work to support herself and her daughter. Then she was shuttled from one home to another. Some of those Chinese antiques now grace my sister's and my homes.

Now the stories and perhaps the myths of Mama's origins, fed stories by Grandma Esther, gave her a sense of being different. Was her father born in England? Did he indeed send those Chinese objects to Grandma Esther?

Mama, the Diva, was always at odds with the siblings who were born after Esther remarried. Were those stories of my mother and her father a myth? Did Mama pass on the diva attitude to me and also to my sister?

The diva attitude. Always perfect, perfect. Hats and gloves on the way to the butcher. And I? Perfect long dark curls and perfect stylish clothes combined with perfect manners. Was this in the genes?

As a young child I clearly remember visiting my great grand-parents Sherman in their apartment in the Bronx. The house smelled of chicken soup and the herring Great Grandpa Sherman liked with dark rye bread for breakfast.

But most astonishing to me was tea time when we would come to visit. I still remember the details. Tea and small cakes would appear on a table set with a handmade doily as Grandpa Sherman raised a glass of amber whiskey and shouted, "To the Queen!" Where was Great Grandma Sherman? Standing quietly next to him, a shadow.

And what about my mother? While she seemed fragile, she could be as strong as tempered steel and could take charge of any situation no matter how tough it was. Was that leadership? Do I have a sprinkle of those genes?

My dad couldn't care less about fashion or clothing. Getting him to shop for himself had been impossible! But Mama took charge. Off she would go to Marshall Field's with a sample of his clothes for size, and buy him outfits from inside out! He was the same way with cars. Running board (I remember them!) falling off? Rusty fenders? As long as it ran he didn't care.

"I don't need all this, but thanks," he says, as he glances at their bed with all the new clothes set out before him. Kiss, hug time.

"And that's not all I bought," Mama gloats, testing her power. Women did not do or say the things Mama did and said back then!

"I bought a new car today!"

"You didn't, did you?" Dad asks. But he already knows the answer. World War II was over and new cars had begun rolling off the line again, although in limited quantities.

"Over the phone, I suppose?" Mama did not have a driver's license yet.

"Yep. Pick it up tomorrow."

"Ruthie," he then says, "why? The one we have still works."

"Good enough for now is just like your clothes!" Her voice is rising.

"Allie, would you please excuse us for a minute?" He makes it sound like a command.

I leave, shutting the door behind me as I realize that kiss and hug time is over.

So if she was so fragile, where did she get the spunk and the chutzpah to do some of the things she did?

———

Funny, isn't it, how memory plays out in your head and heart? Or is it the stories and myths handed down and told over and over at family dinners and gatherings that I remember?

It surprises me now that I didn't think anything of it in Grandma Rahmey's house that all my aunts and Grandma herself took part in businesses that were run by Grandpa Eli and his brother Jack Rahmey.

Did I inherit my business acumen and salesmanship from those aunts and Grandma herself? Or did I just absorb all they said, their actions, the visits to their stores? Once again I question the genes and the myths!

More memories. But for a short time I did know Grandma Rahmey's mother. My great grandmother, who we called Siti, which means grandmother in Arabic. I remember a tiny toothless woman sitting on a pile of cushions in Grandma Rahmey's living room smoking a narguile, a water pipe. And her little bull dog, who only understood Arabic.

And once again I wonder, what was in that water pipe? She did smile a lot! I smile a lot, but I don't have a water pipe!

I think I am a composite of all my aunts, grandmas, Mama and a few sprinkles of the men in my life as well. A product of two cultures and the best of two worlds. I'm thankful for the women I came from, either fact or fiction…myths of often-told tales.

"So, Grandma Rahmey," I ask silently today, looking at those pictures, "Did you pass on to me this willful streak, this strong independence, and most of your recipes? Are you the one who gave me this bosom? Were the street smarts and backbone of my father passed from you to him and on to me?"

I like to think she did pass all that on to me. Too bad she died so young. To this day I lament the fact that I never got answers to the questions about her family and where she came from.

———

Within the Syrian Jewish community in Brooklyn today, Rahmey is still a proud name. After years, decades and generations, it seems to still carry respect and dignity. I forgot to mention, Grandpa Eli Rahmey was one of the founders of a synagogue in Brooklyn in the early 1920s as an influx of Syrian Jews sought a better life in a new country. The family originated in Damascus, but my dad was born in Beirut.

Syrian Jews upon arriving in America joined the thousands of European Jews already living on the Lower East side of New York. But they were different. They were dark, they did not speak Yiddish. They spoke Arabic and French and they ate strange food. No herring and black bread for them.

So who am I? Alice Joan Rahmey-Borodkin-Brodsky. What a mouthful.

Grandma Sophia and Grandpa Eli Rahmey
Wedding in Damascus

11

Who Am I?

Alice and Arnie's Wedding

By marrying the boy next door, I became a Borodkin and was steeped in the Russian traditions, language and food of that country. Surrounded by classical music and what seemed like a million competing cousins.

But still I was Alice Joan Rahmey.

After forty-seven years as Alice Borodkin, I found myself widowed and thought, "Well, now I am no longer a Borodkin. I am Alice Rahmey."

As fate would have it, I met and married another man. Arnold Brodsky, another Russian! Later, I ran for office on the name Borodkin because that's what everyone knew me as, Alice Borodkin. Confused? It gets worse. Most people could hardly say Borodkin, let alone Borodkin-Brodsky. So I kept the Borodkin name and filed my election papers.

That created confusion within the Democratic party in Colorado as well. Suddenly late at night during my quest for office I receive a phone call from the Denver Dems.

"Alice, you are not a registered Democrat! You can't run for office!" they said.

"Not to worry," I assured them. "Look under Brodsky, my legal name." They did, they found me and I served for eight years.

So once again I wonder. Who am I? It seems to me I will always be Alice Joan Rahmey underneath all the other names and titles.

A sort of world-weary traveler. A Syrian Jew on my dad's side, with an American mother, Russian in-laws, and generations of mixed genes and emotions. And of course my own special DNA.

———

Mama, like her mother, Grandma Esther Gottlieb, was born in New York City. Mama was blond and thin compared to my father, dark and handsome—a Rudolph Valentino lookalike. Mama's side of the family, no matter that all of them were born here in America, was not that much different than the Syrian side. Like all families they argued about everything, had strong opinions and, I now recognize, a strong streak of integrity.

In those days in New York and Chicago, all families lived in very close proximity to each other. Either upstairs, downstairs or around the corner. And only one family had a phone! Perhaps it was this close proximity that caused all that friction…and gossip that became the stuff of my life.

European Jews, with their penchant for education, could not imagine or understand the energy, planning and discussions that went on around the clock as these newcomers hustled and opened businesses on nothing but their guts and chutzpah. They opened factories in China, manufactured linens and began import-export businesses. Where and how they raised the money to start this new life is still a mystery to me.

It never occurred to me growing up that such a small community had so many factions. There were the Syrian Jews from Aleppo and Damascus, and the Lebanese Jews from Lebanon. And those considered Sephardim, from Spain and Portugal...mostly Jews from Spain who were forced out of their country during the Spanish inquisition and fled to the Middle East. Jews from Damascus and Aleppo speak French, Hebrew and Arabic. Sephardim Jews speak Spanish, Ladino and Hebrew.

Grandma Rahmey often warned me about staying away from "lower class" Syrian Jews from Aleppo. And she often stated, Jews from Baghdad had purple lips and could not be trusted! Can't believe that I grew up so liberal.

So what do we have? We have Syrian Jews who migrated to the New World and established themselves. And a divide frequently persisted between those with roots in Aleppo, the Halibi Jews, and Damascus, the Shami Jews.

This split persists to present day, with each community maintaining some cultural institutions and organizations, and to a lesser extent, a preference for in-group marriage. But over time intermarriage has blended them all and the community seems all the same to me.

On a recent trip to Israel, our tour guide asked me if I was a Shami or a Halabi. I started to answer him and he interrupted me saying, "You are definitely a Shami!"

"How did you know I was an Arabic Jew at all?" I asked.

"I can just tell," he answered.

I always thought I was an American of Syrian descent or, as my Dad would correct me, Lebanese descent.

———————

So where did I get my penchant for cooking? Perhaps Grandma Rahmey had something to do with it.

Grandma Rahmey. The delightful aroma of her Sunday cooking filled not only the house, but the neighborhood and left an indelible imprint in my mind.

No matter whether it was a holiday dinner or just a Sunday family gathering, I was immediately ushered into the steaming kitchen and fed my favorite foods. Today we call it Pita bread. To me it was Syrian bread filled to the brim with meatballs simmered in tomato sauce, cumin, allspice, tarragon and other delectable spices.

And if no one was looking a small cup of Turkish coffee and some wonderful sweet cake just out of the oven. I loved it then and I love it so much now that I continue to cook her favorite foods from handed down recipes.

12

The Chink in the Samovar

Abe Borodkin, Composer, Conductor, Cellist

Now let's add in the Russians. Cultural tensions were always there, it seemed, but for various reasons. How I enjoyed those dinners at my husband Howard's home before and after we were married. A Russian dinner to fill the stomach, with blini, borsht and plenty of vodka. When my family and I would arrive, there would be a big oval table set up in his mother's dining room. It was spread with herring, pickles, rye bread, tomatoes and boiled potatoes. And that was just the appetizer!

Immediately after dinner everyone took out their violin, clarinet or cello or sat around the piano to entertain us with beautiful music.

That's when I could see my mother turn to stone. Although I didn't realize it then, her change of mood was because she was no longer the center of attention.

The two families, soon to be joined by my marriage to Howard, were as culturally different as high tide and low tide. To the Russians it seemed that my Syrian Jewish father and my American-English mother were from another world.

My parents enjoyed the symphony and good books and strove mightily to make their eldest daughter a "lady." At this point I was taking music lessons, horseback lessons, drama lessons, along with those ballet lessons. Neither of my parents had made it to college. My father had dropped out of high school to help the family financially during the Depression. Now I understand his constant need to read and his thirst for classical music. Books and music albums had filled our library walls. Much to the chagrin of my mother, who would have preferred to fill those shelves with Chinese antiques.

Dad read to me from Longfellow and taught me to read before I was five and entered school. Mom took me to the symphony and the museums. But no college degrees.

Other differences between the two families: Mama was most fond of her brandy. My in-laws, except for having vodka at dinner, did not drink at all. Mother's clothes were the latest fashion and her whole persona was one of, yes, perfection. Howard's mother was a conservative dresser, but always in style. The two houses were immaculate as they both followed the script as well. Surely there were copies of Betty Crocker in their kitchens!

Once Howard and I married, however, it became clear that I would be the one to host all the holiday family dinners. I did Mother's Day, Father's Day, Jewish high holidays and anything else nobody knew where to celebrate. If we wanted peace in the family this was the way to go. We did not choose one family over the other to celebrate with. My friends later commented that their Christian holidays were similar.

But as I see it, dinners at my house weren't neutral territory. The families liked coming to my home for these occasions. It was my cooking. My preparation. My presentation. And I ate it up! Waiting as all entered my home for those words of praise… "What a beautiful table!" "What delicious food!" "And your beautiful children and you." All so pretty and well groomed…I was my mother!

We heard a lot of history from the other side of the family during those days. Mina Borodkin, my mother-in-law, according to family stories, came from an educated musical and business-oriented family in Russia. My favorite story was about the buried gold. According to family myth, although everyone swore it was true, Mina's father had started an electric company in their village near Minsk in Russia and buried a treasure in gold under a tree near their home. I heard that story over and over again and never thought to ask questions about it. *The Good Wife Book* had probably told me to be quiet and not interrupt!

Years and generations later, my sister-in-law, Sue, her daughter, Marni, and my son Steven, who by then was in his late forties, traveled to that village to check out this story. In fact a PBS video team, alerted by Sue, accompanied them after hearing about the gold. They did find the house and the tree. But no buried treasure!

Mina would regale us with stories of her school days, when a young Vladimir Horowitz—who was a friend of Mina's and who many called the village nerd—according to her stories, would dash home each day after school to practice into the night on his piano.

Her stories about Horowitz didn't stop there. It seems the two families had all emigrated to the United States and stayed friends for years. According to Mina, Horowitz was a womanizer and remained one after he married the conductor Leopold Stokowski's daughter. "Very strange child and stranger as he grew older," she told us.

The sisters in Mina's family were real redheads. Luba, Asya and Mina. From their old pictures, I know they must have been gorgeous, and they still were when I met them so many years later.

Other stories were not so funny. That PBS video, which featured the families' backgrounds, was my first glimpse of life in Russia at the turn of the century. Not a ghetto or a shtetl, but a village of semi-prominent Jews and Christians. Although they were living side by side, shopping in the same markets, taking piano lessons from a young Mina, trouble for Jews was right around the corner at all times.

So the story goes, Mina's father, Jacob, gave the village priest large donations for the church in order to secure his promise to let them know if a pogrom—violent attacks on Jews in the Russian empire—was about to take place.

Pogroms were common in the late 1800s and all through the early and middle 1900s. Cossacks from the Czar's army would sweep through the villages and murder, rape and destroy as many Jewish homes, businesses and schools as they could. So, the story goes, the priest knew in advance and would hide the red-headed sisters in the church basement.

Those sisters were quite a team. Arguing over this and that, Asya could never make up her mind about anything...and Luba? Well, Luba loved her husband Costia more then anything in the world, except for her children, Rona and Robert. Luba always reminded me of Khrushchev's wife and was pretty plump! Mina was the typical wife of the forties and stayed that way until she died at age 102.

Very few escaped getting Russian nicknames. Rona became Ronitchka, Robert just became Bobby and my Howard was called Hotche, after a candy that Asya loved. My sister-in-law Sue became Susanky. I was always Alice. I felt, it should have been, Just Alice.

Every year, our big event was always the Jewish holiday of Rosh Hashanah. The Jewish New Year. Family used to come from all over and those with no place to go were welcome as well.

I always called that holiday The Great Matzo Ball Event. Every year we repeated the same story, with the same cast of characters.

My mother-in-law, Mina, known to all as Minichka, was exactly what a housewife in the 1940s and 1950s was supposed to be. No matter the day, she always was freshly dressed and groomed by 7:00 a.m. as she prepared breakfast for her family. And every year she was in charge of making the matzo balls for the chicken soup.

Her Jewish high holiday dinners were very traditional Eastern European. Chicken soup and matzo balls, roast chicken and potatoes, and honey cake for a sweet New Year.

The matzo balls were the high point of the year in her house. Her sisters, Luba and Asya, and their families would be in attendance as Mina began the process. Everyone had something to say...

More Matzo meal, one egg, no two, don't forget the oil, grease your hands, be sure the water is boiling. If it was me, I would have thrown them all out of the kitchen. My mother-in-law was a real redhead. As were her sisters. Luba was always dieting. But she was the official matzo ball taster.

"Oy, Minitchka," she would say, "These are wonderful! But I am on a diet and I will only eat three today!" This after testing three or four before dinner.

Asya was the youngest and the most beautiful of the sisters. She was slim and had the face of a woman who took great care of her appearance. "Meena," she would say, "these matzo balls are so big… please make them more delicate." As if her mouth was a small perfect rose bud that could not open wide enough to accommodate the plump matzo ball.

Every year it was the same. When dinner was over, everyone took out their musical instruments and played pieces from operas, or perhaps something they'd composed. My father-in-law would play the cello, and assorted cousins would play the violin, the clarinet (my husband) and the piano.

Mina would just watch and listen, although she was a fine pianist. Perhaps the Great Matzo Ball Event wore her out.

Cooking matzo balls and chicken soup, and preparing a holiday dinner always makes me a bit sad. But it also makes me happy that I had those Great Matzo Ball Experiences. As the years passed and each of the parents grew a bit older, it fell to me to make those dinners. My Thanksgiving dinners were and still are amazing feats of cooking and eating that take several days of preparation. In fact, after moving to Denver from New York, my sister-in law Sue, who rarely cooked, sent tickets to our family to fly back to New York so I could make an Alice Thanksgiving Dinner.

I always started with a fresh turkey, not a frozen one. Seasoned inside and out with just about every herb and flavorable spice I could think of. Fresh tarragon, dill, chives, shallots, cumin, allspice, garlic, salt and pepper and a shot of cinnamon. It would rest in the refrigerator overnight. Hopefully absorbing those magnificent flavors.

The stuffing was prepared with onions and garlic browned in olive oil. One-day-old French bread was diced and toasted and added to the onions and garlic. Chickpeas and one egg were then added and stirred together. Into and around the turkey it went.

Of course there was the salad, the fresh vegetables and the Middle Eastern Mezza—olives, grape leaves and string cheese with olive oil and lemon splashed and dashed over the plate. By the time we got to dessert, most people had made a mad dash to the nearest couch, chair or floor with open belts and zippers.

And I, a twenty-something married woman now with a small baby, who thought this was what and how I should be acting. And acting was exactly what it was for me.

In all that noise and confusion of family, I felt unseen and unheard.

I am not sure why I had those feelings back then. The gatherings were friendly enough, and I certainly got raves about my cooking and table setting when I took over those holidays. But there seemed to be a cloud I couldn't shake off. I have such clear memories of those times … there we were, all crammed into the small kitchen with those white, hard to wash, starched and ironed curtains. The drama of cooking this special meal surrounded me. Mina would always ask, "How is the chicken soup?" "How is the brisket?" "What should I put into the salad?" Lots of chattering and I guess love.

Mina and Mama were both my role models of a sort during those years. Mina was Mina. Mama the Diva was beautiful and well-dressed as she cooked and cleaned and took care of my dad. But that's where the Norman Rockwell painting ended. At those events and at home, Mama was outspoken and stubborn as she sipped her ever-present brandy. Perhaps seeing her in contrast to Mina brought that tinge of sadness to these occasions for me. Without having that comparison, I didn't have to think about the flaws.

———————

In one big way, these mothers were much the same: they were under the influence of Betty Crocker. Both mothers rose early every morning, dressed, with makeup on, of course, set the table for everyone's breakfast, a real breakfast! Followed by cleaning the house, every day, and believe it or not, my mother-in-law even ironed Abrasha's shorts!

And there I was, "Diva in Training, Betty Crocker's Future," sitting smashed up against the kitchen wall, feeding my young son. By the way, the chair at the kitchen table became the chair we all used when feeding our kids over the years.

But a bit of Betty Friedan, even years before *The Feminine Mystique*, always would sneak into my thoughts: "What's the big deal about cooking a dinner? You don't need to ask anyone, just do it!" Me, bucking the system quietly.

13

My Russian Chapter

The Fishbergs and Borodkins

The two most numerous musical families in the U.S. are the Fishberg-Glantzes and the Borodkin-Gusikoffs. Spread from Hollywood to Manhattan, with relatives in half the major symphony orchestras of the U.S., these two strains of musicians could each constitute a sizable orchestra. Collectively, they constitute one of the most impressive genealogical phenomena ever studied outside of Boston.

The simple statistics are arresting. Among the Fishbergs and Glantzes there

haired wife Fannie in a little three-room apartment in Brooklyn. Isaac is a flutist.

Last week Isaac conducted the Fishberg family's Passover services with true patriarchal dignity. Fishbergs from Manhattan and The Bronx, with their wives and children, put away their fiddles and trombones to visit him in Brooklyn. Vigorous, blue-eyed Isaac, his grey, cropped hair covered with a black skullcap, looked them over sharply. Isaac (by a previous wife) had begotten so many children he could hardly keep track of them. Of a total of 16, ten—Arriga, Theodore, Jascha, Wil-

ISAAC FISHBERG
He is the 94-year-old patriarch of the most musical family in the U.S.

Liza-Graphic House

are in the U.S. (and Russia has more): ten violinists, eight trumpeters, three pianists, two flutists, two clarinetists, two saxophonists, two drummers and one double bassist. Among the Borodkins and Gusikoffs there are five cellists, two violinists, four trumpeters, two drummers, one violist, one pianist, one clarinetist and one trombonist. The total amounts to some 47 orchestra players, includes twelve violinists, twelve trumpet players. Among the most prominent are Mischa Mischakoff (real name Fishberg), concertmaster of the NBC Symphony; Harry Glantz, first trumpet of the NBC Symphony; Sidney Baker (a Fishberg), first trumpet of the Chicago Symphony;* Charles Gusikoff, first trombone of the Philadelphia Orchestra; Saul Caston (a Gusikoff), assistant conductor of the Philadelphia Orchestra.

Isaac, the Patriarch. The Gusikoffs are an old Moscow family tracing themselves with pride to Michael Gusikoff (1806-37), great pioneer virtuoso on the xylophone. The Borodkins are from Minsk and have known, and intermarried with, the Gusikoffs only since both arrived in the U.S. The Fishbergs and Glantzes, however, knew one another intimately in the Ukranian town of Proskurov where Pincas Glantz and Isaac Fishberg played in the local band under the Czars. The patriarch Isaac Fishberg, 94, is still as spry as a Bessarabian goat. He lives with his grey-
* Now with the U.S. armed forces.

liam, Mischa, Pearl, Lisa, Bessie, Rebecca and Fishel—were in the U.S. Ten grandchildren were either professional musicians or on the way to that calling. Isaac's favorite son is Mischa Mischakoff, who earns about $25,000 a year.

Pink-cheeked Isaac Fishberg speaks only Yiddish and is a man of great spirit. In spite of his age, he gets up at 4 o'clock every morning to visit the synagogue, does the family marketing himself on the way home. He is infuriated if anyone suggests that his health is delicate. He has high blood pressure, but claims to enjoy it. He views most of his in-laws with tolerance, but would not live with any of his descendants for a prophet's ransom.

Two weeks ago 94-year-old Isaac Fishberg came home after a night out and had to be put to bed because of a serious nosebleed. He refused to tell where he had been. The truth finally leaked out. Bored with the routine of domestic life, Isaac had sneaked away with his flute to a Jewish wedding where he had played for four hours at a stretch.

Time Magazine Article about the Borodkin Family

*T*ime magazine on February 16, 1957 published an article naming the Borodkins as one of the families with the most relatives in the music industry. In a way it also is a story of how I came to know the family, those next-door neighbors whose name I would ultimately bear.

How I received a copy of that article is yet another event in what turns out to be a jam-packed life. As my sister Ellen remarked recently, "Alice, you have so many stories to be told. Tell them."

I like to think of my life as chapters. This one is my Russian chapter, Part Two. It starts in Denver, Colorado…

While serving in the Colorado Legislature from 2001 to 2009, I attended a conference held by Women's Legislative Lobby. The conference actually was in Washington, DC. Since all of us were wearing name tags, it was easy to spot names. A legislator in Massachusetts approached me and asked, "Are you related to Lucy and Linda Borodkin? It's not a common name, you know."

Suddenly I was thrown back fifty or more years to a small summer camp in the Catskills Mountains of New York, run by Ethel and Misha Borodkin, my husband's aunt and uncle. Misha was a violinist with the New York Philharmonic under the direction of Leonard Bernstein. I was never sure what Ethel did besides running the camp. I still hear Misha saying, "You know, we call him Lenny."

Linda and Lucy as well as my nine year old sister-in-law Suzanne Toma Borodkin, a Russian name she quickly changed by dropping the Toma when she was older, all attended the summer camp. As newlyweds, Howard and I joined my mother-in-law Mina and father-in law Abrasha in a trip to visit Sue at the camp as part of a family gathering.

That was the first and last time I met Lucy and Linda and one of the last times I saw Misha. A family feud had been going on for many years and finally the boiling point blew it apart.

How far back did the issue go? As the story goes and how I heard it, in the 1920s the Borodkins left Russia for the United States to avoid anti-Semitism and pogroms. Abrasha's father, I was told, was a violinist in the Czar's army…quite an achievement for a Jew in those days, so they were relatively well-off, but far from safe from those that raided their village in Minsk.

Abrasha's father died in Germany from pneumonia. So his wife, Anastasia Borodkin, who told people that she was the lost Anastasia of the Royal Russian family, even though she was Jewish, along with her children and her big brass Samovar, an urn used to heat water for tea, dated 1863—which now graces my dining room—went from Russia to Germany to Turkey and finally to America.

Arriving in a strange country, with young siblings Manya, Misha, Ria, and Mira, being the oldest, Abrasha was in charge of their life.

Like many immigrant families, he had to give up his dreams of being a composer and conductor in order to be sure his siblings would continue their education. He was a fine cellist. He was able to make a living in night clubs during the era of prohibition. Later in life he was able to achieve his own dreams.

He composed and conducted at Carnegie Hall. Among other music he had written a cantata, "Here Oh Israel." I have the original music with his cigar burn marks and ink splotches on the composition paper. I picture him now sitting at the baby grand piano in the house next door, chomping on that cigar, holding back his bushy gray hair in one hand while he wrote and rewrote that music.

While Misha went on building his career to become a violinist and the others pursued various careers, all in the music industry, resentment lay curled in Abrasha's heart.

Misha and Abrasha clashed over how much they contributed to the care of Babushka Nastia, their mother, and how much Abrasha had to give up to care for the family. It's an old story of families split over values and perceived hurts. Babushka is a Russian word for grandmother. You see them from time to time in pictures from old Russia with woolen scarves tied neatly under their ample chins to keep warm. But not Anastasia Borodkin. To her, everyone was "common." I must have been uncommon as I was accepted into the family with open arms.

As the story goes, Anastasia led everyone she knew down the garden path with her mystery and her hints about who she really was—Anastasia, the supposedly only child of the Czar and Czarina of Russia who escaped the family assassinations. She spoke in Russian of her summer gardens and winter gardens, and her beloved cat, who I never actually saw nor did anyone else when we went to visit her. She needed to be reminded that she was Jewish and therefore could not be the Czar's daughter.

And, by the way, only Russian was permitted in the house. No English and absolutely no Yiddish. Of course the younger Borodkins learned English quickly if they expected to thrive in their new country. I understand the Yiddish restriction as that would have given away their Jewish heritage. But, according to Babushka, the language was too common for their so-called cultural standing.

———

Now here I was, confronted with the news that Lucy and Linda are close friends of the woman who asked me if I knew them. Would I like to get in touch with them, she asked? You bet! I replied. And so it began.

First, a very tentative phone call to Lucy. My God, when did we get so old? I was just twenty when I visited the camp to watch them on the swim team. Now here we were discussing the family dynamics, the breast cancer the sisters had hopefully beaten and the recent death of my sister-in-law Sue at sixty from that dreaded malady.

When Lucy sent me the *Time* magazine article it brought back the times we spent in Carnegie Hall and the late night dinners in the original Russian Tea Room. It's hard to imagine that tea room on West 57th Street is eighty-five years old this year. And so many people with the same last name Borodkin, cousins and family all related in some fashion…

———

We are at the Russian Tea Room in New York City next door to Carnegie Hall. The old, old Russian Tea Room with the cane-back chairs and the black and white tiled floors, surrounded by brass Samovars filled with hot water or tea. Abrasha has just conducted his cantata to a full house.

Russian is the language of the evening. Most of the musicians had fled Russia in the 1920s as the Borodkins had. We arrive in a limo, which my father-in-law has provided for my family and his, and we are dropped off near the stage door on Fifty-Seventh Street in Manhattan, as I recall, in a soft spring rain.

The women in our party hurry from the car door to the stage door, afraid they might ruin their hair in the rain. In the 1940s and 50s, everyone was, as they say, dressed to the teeth, whatever that meant.

I wear a pink linen sleeveless dress with genuine imitation diamonds around the neck. And, of course, hat and gloves. The men remind me of marching penguins in their black and white tuxedoes.

The concert was great but the real show is the Russian Tea Room. So much vodka, hugging, kissing and back-slapping. A bit of musical critique is thrown in as well if you listen closely.

I am too young to appreciate those friends of Abrasha. It seems to me then that they were some sort of brotherhood. A community of talented Russians recreating their homeland, their music, and their political views and stimulating intelligent arguments.

I was fourteen or fifteen at the time, but since we were living next door to my musician future husband, my family and I were always invited to attend the various musical events.

I was too young to appreciate those who came and went from the Borodkin home…most friends of my father-in-law. I remember Aaron Copland, Morton Gould, Zero Mostel.

Such stories!

14

"Alice Dinners"

Perfect Table

I have a confession to make. I loved cooking those dinners for family and for company. It was never a chore. I still love it. It has a calming effect on me. The symphony softly playing…Oscar, the dog, asleep in the sun, except when he is begging to taste my cooking…the preparation of food, watching as the perfect rice is prepared…or that luscious roasting chicken…and of course chicken soup filling the house with smells of a home. The aroma of allspice, cumin, cinnamon or onions simmering in olive oil. Comfort to me anyway; not sure how the rest of the family feels. But they sure enjoy the food!

All these fragrances fill me with so many memories. Family dinners, dubbed the "Alice Dinners" by sister-in-law Sue, who loved having dinner at our house. Although my mother-in-law was a good cook, Sue felt there was more "flair," as she put it, at my house. And more fun, she added later on. True, my in-laws were very Russian. And Mina and Abrasha were prone to sadness. Perhaps, I sometimes think, the sadness was why my father-in law's music was so beautiful.

Alice Dinners. What made them so special? The way the table was set? Always with a beautiful linen tablecloth, matching napkins— remember, we had to iron them in those days—the colorful dishes with the brown and yellow flowers, and the amber glasses next to my grandmother's crystal wine glasses, which I still use to this day.

Company or not, I tried to set a version of that table every night. It pleased me to do so. Dinners were just good solid food. Meatloaf, mashed potatoes, a fresh vegetable, a salad, rolls and dessert. On some occasions, a roast beef, rare of course, as we all liked it. Or, perhaps simply meatballs and spaghetti, with my special tomato and wine sauce.

And then there were my Thanksgiving dinners, which took me several days to cook, but only about half an hour for guests to gobble up.

One Thanksgiving dinner stands out clearly. As usual it was at our house. Wouldn't have it any other way. It was memorable because it was the first Thanksgiving that Ellen and her new husband, Harry, and my sister-in law Sue and her new husband, Harold, attended along with assorted parents and friends.

My dad was so proud of the turkey, he hopped into the kitchen, picked up the bird on a silver platter and held it high up in the air for all to see. Well, the turkey slipped off the platter, skidded across the dining room floor, and ended up in the living room. Howard observed the thirty second rule, grabbed the slightly battered turkey and put it back on the platter. No problem as he carved our dinner.

Another "Alice dinner" was started. Only this time it was a long-distance preparation. Daily long distance calls from Sue, who hardly ever cooked. What kind of turkey? How big? Frozen or fresh? What else should I buy? How about dessert? And on and on it went for weeks.

Since Sue and I had decided to have a frozen turkey one year, I called her in New York several days before we were to arrive reminding her to defrost it. Years afterward we were still laughing about that event, she remembered the defrosting but forgot to take the package of gizzards out before cooking it!

Now life has changed. It's a constant factor for all of us. My parents are gone, my in-laws are gone, and husband of forty-seven years is gone. So too my sister-in-law Sue. But as the cooking circle of life goes on, I cook for a new husband, my daughter, once in a great while my son, grandson and daughter-in-law when I go to New York and many friends who have become extended family. I still set the table every night, even if it is just the two of us. But now I light romantic candles. I also still cook on Sundays so we have what we need for the upcoming busy week.

But really I cook for the memories and just because I love to cook.

15

When the Unimaginable Actually Happened

Happier Days, 1951.
Daddy, Alice, Ellen, Howard

I t seems I cannot get through a Thanksgiving dinner without remembering the sliding turkey and my dad's laughter. But there are so many other memories. For instance, when I was young, I had pneumonia twice and during those times I was in the hospital I worried about my dolls—I had a large collection—as a mother would worry over her children. They were my children.

Mama had a cedar chest which she kept in my room that stood against the wall opposite my bed. The chest had about twelve dolls on it, each a present from my dad—each a beautiful Madame Alexander baby doll or slightly more grown-up fancy dressed doll, all with beautiful faces.

My babies. Each came with a wardrobe of dresses and night clothes, baby bottles and a little trunk to keep them in. I think my dad, knowing how much I cared for the dolls, had as much joy picking them out as I did in loving them.

Each evening I would start at one end of the chest, undress each doll, wash, change into nightgowns and lay them down under the cover Mama had crocheted for them. In the morning I repeated the ritual and dressed them for the day. I was about seven or eight.

Here's the point. That time when I had pneumonia, I could hardly breathe or move but I was worried about my children. Dad would perform the ritual of covering and uncovering my babies every morning and evening before he left to open our hosiery store and immediately after he came home each night.

To me this represents the essence of the Betty Crocker era, when a little girl would be encouraged to care for and play with her little kitchen oven and pots and pans and dolls. After all, this was her future. Practice couldn't hurt. Yes, girls still play with dolls now but they also have baseball bats and skateboards that are just as much a part of them. My dolls were my life.

Ironically, in some ways Dad perpetuated the myth of what my future *a la* Betty Crocker would or should be. In other ways he expected more from me and always encouraged me to join in his business ventures.

When I was on that train headed to New York with Mama during the war, I know Dad never forgot to cover my dolls and that had made me happy. It also made me happy learning the business and being in the stores with Daddy.

Confusing, wasn't it?

Loss comes to all of us. It takes many shapes. Loss of life, loss of a job, loss of health. Loss is a process of life. But we never think of loss when we are young. Life will last forever and nothing will change… right?

The phone rang around 8:00 p.m. on an evening of the usual—dinner, homework, bath and bed for Steven and Julie and then quiet time.

Can I remember who called? Yes. It was a neighbor and friend of my parents.

"Alice?"

"Yes?" I said to the voice.

"It's your dad. He just had a heart attack and he's dead."

The unimaginable had happened. I suppose my face gave away the message before I cried out, as my husband raced toward me.

"What? Who died? What happened?"

Stricken as I was with hot painful tears, "My dad," I managed to say.

"I'll go," Howard said, "you stay with the kids."

The unimaginable had happened and I stayed home? What was I thinking? No goodbye? No final hug and kiss? No daddy smell of cigars and shaving lotion? He was only sixty-nine. We still had so much more time. He had just opened a manufacturing plant, he was planning on taking the kids to the park tomorrow.

When the phone rang again, I jumped. What more and devastating news could there be?

It was my mother-in-law, in her soft Russian accent.

"Dahling!"

Please don't, I thought. I cannot bear any kind words now.

I don't remember the children coming to me, I don't remember their tears. They simply loved him.

It was December and Julie our daughter was ten. Grandpa Moe had bought her a winter jacket with "real" fur around the hood. She kept that jacket until her mid-twenties. I kept other memories.

16

A Baby's Gift

Baby Julie, 2 weeks old, with Alice

Today as I cook my mind drifts to so many memories of dinners cooked for family or friends. Those dinners were bright with conversation and jokes and good food. Leg of lamb and rice seasoned with Middle Eastern spices, good wine, and a beautiful presentation. Perfect!

But, I have to admit some of those family gatherings were not the happy experiences I make them out to be. Families can be troublesome with hidden agendas: real or imagined past incidents simmering just below the surface, like a stew bubbling away. Why is it that gatherings like these sometimes bring these issues to the front?

Although most of our family dinners together were pleasant, one stands out as devastating. At the time Steven was age fifteen and Julie was seven. I believe a bunch of assorted aunts, uncles and cousins were there.

Julie was adopted and she knew it. Everyone in the family knew it, and everyone has loved and accepted her since she arrived as a three-day-old, red-faced squirming bundle.

At one of those family dinners it stunned everyone at the table, then, when an aunt asked me about having another baby. She knew that I'd had several miscarriages and a still-born after Steven was born. Wanting more children, Howard and I had finally made the decision to adopt. After I reminded her of the reason we had Julie, she said, "Oh. Who wants someone else's dirty laundry?"

That remark sent Julie running from the table, trailed quickly by her father and me and her grandparents, all rushing to calm her tears and tell her how we all adored her. Not exactly a family dinner we enjoyed!

Now I see cooking did not always work the way I wanted it to. A bit late in life, I came to realize that filling the stomach does not make *everything* better. Nor does a perfect meal guarantee that everyone will act in a loving manner. The cooking, I was coming to realize, is just one way to go deeper to fill the heart and soul and mind to try to have harmony reign.

Over the years, when I would be in a creative cooking and thinking mode, I often thought of Julie. Our Julie. A pretty wonderful happening in our family's life cycle of events. In the days before Julie had arrived and before I even knew she existed, I cooked and cooked as if to heal myself from the constant pain of loss of those children I would never have. I don't remember if I enjoyed the actual cooking or not, or if family dinners were fun or stressful back then. How could I not see the suffering of Howard and our son?

Then Julie arrived. I thought our family complete and I would be happily roused out of my depression by a crying newborn. A blond blue-eyed son, an olive skinned baby girl with light brown curls. What more could I ask for?

But as Julie grew older I wondered what had happened to her that was causing her to slip into the underworld of dark depression I knew so well. Perhaps she saw what I could not or would not see. The underlying tension between my husband and me. The surface tension between my husband and his father. The just under the surface tension between my family and my husband's family. Perhaps my lack of satisfaction with my life, a feeling of being pulled in two directions away from the real me bled over to her.

I so vividly recall the morning of her adoption. Howard and I were dressing to go to court and hear the judge say, "I now declare Julie Borodkin yours now and forever!" And with a bang of the judge's gavel, something we already knew…Julie would be ours!

In New York during the 1960s the adoption law stated that the biological parents had the right to change their mind and ask for the baby's return within three months. We sweated out those three months with Howard ready to grab Steven and Julie and me and run to Canada if necessary.

No need. The biological mother was flown to New York from Maryland and signed the proper papers. That part was over.

Then one more step—a visit from a Human Services counselor to make sure all was well in the family. We never knew when that visit would occur. But in my usual fashion, every day, I made the bed, got dressed and "put my face on," dressed the baby, sent Steven off to school, put up the coffee and waited….and went out to shop for food…and waited some more!

And then one morning the doorbell rang and there she was, files, pen and smile.

Well, by this time Julie, still not entirely "ours," was almost a year old and came toddling up to see who had come to visit. Brown curls bobbing, overalls and blouse in place, and smile ready for whomever it was. And the dreaded interview was over before I could even offer coffee! A quick look around the apartment, a peek into Julie's room and the woman was gone! No questions, no problems.

But back up, the story wasn't all that simple. What adoption story is? When we first set out to adopt, we learned that the laws of those days in the sixties were strict. So strict it could have been that we'd apply and then wait for two, three years or more just to meet with a counselor. The reason for this wait? If you were Jewish, or as they said on the application form, "Hebrew," the only agency you could adopt from was the Louis B Weiss Jewish Adoption Services. Not like today when you can adopt as a single parent, same-sex partnership, white to black and black to white and just about any religion.

A friend of ours then told me we could work around the system, still be legal and go through a lawyer. She gave us a name; we called and made an appointment to speak to him.

Oh, yes. We could adopt a baby. However, we would have to pay for the mother's care and hospital bill, his fee, and myriad other items. The total was way outside our budget. We left. Again I felt that feeling of loss, as if there had been a baby and it had nearly been mine. No wonder I was depressed. I was becoming obsessed with loss.

A few weeks later our phone rang late on a Friday evening in October. Fate or some mysterious hand had sent a baby to us. The lawyer asked if we were still interested in adopting. Of course I said yes.

The situation was this: a baby girl who was promised to another couple, who were in London at the time, was born early and the couple could not return to the US in time to claim her.

"Don't worry about the money," the lawyer said. "She was three weeks early and is already home. Just pay the hospital bill and come and get her."

The baby was in Maryland. So on the following Monday we hopped on the LaGuardia shuttle between New York and Washington DC and flew off to meet the lawyer, drove to Maryland to pick up the baby and then took the last La Guardia shuttle back to NYC.

I'd had no idea we would have to go to meet the biological parents to get the baby! I was nervous, scared, and thanks to our family doctor, pretty doped up on Valium.

We went to the parents' apartment. There she was. Lying in a dresser drawer ready and waiting for the new, clean baby clothes and beautiful lamb's wool blanket trimmed in pink velvet, and the carefully prepared bottle of formula I had in her baby bag.

I remember that the biological mother was dark, the biological father was a big blond man and there was a three-year-old girl running around. She had blond hair and blue eyes.

I never really made eye contact with either of the parents and only looked at the little girl a little bit. I just wanted to grab my baby and go home.

I'm not even sure that I was conscious of dressing the little five-pound, red and squirming bundle waiting for me to pick up and take home. And it never occurred to me to ask any questions of those two people who had given birth to that baby. Mostly I was desperately afraid I would say or do something that would break the deal, so I kept quiet.

We barely made the last shuttle flight home to New York that evening and the crew on duty remembered seeing us just a few hours earlier boarding the plane.

"My dear," the flight attendant said as she peeked into the blanket, "You must tell me how you did that!"

Meanwhile back home in New York, everyone was anxiously awaiting a glimpse of the new baby. And, just like her grandmother, this child was destined to be outfitted to the hilt.

It was about that time that my dad and I had opened the Little Shop. It was a children's wear shop of high-class clothes. After all, it was located in Forest Hills and the money was there and stylish name-brand baby and toddler clothing were all part of the prestige.

I ended up becoming the buyer for the Little Shop and maneuvered around the garment industry to buy the clothes I thought would fit our market. Julie was not yet ours when I worked there.

When I boarded the plane for Maryland that day, my dad told me not to worry, he would go to the Little Shop that very night and open the store to gather up everything for the baby's layette and bring it to our house. Steven and the baby sitter were there waiting for us and the new member of our family.

It was late at night and cold as well when we got back. No matter. We stopped at my in-laws' house and my parents' house to show them our pink bundle. Everyone was crying happy tears as they pulled the blanket away to take a long look at this baby we called Julie.

Now it's fifty-two years later. And Julie is a grown woman, mature enough to now face looking for her biological parents.

Doesn't bother me at all! We know who her real parents are!

Another Julie story comes to mind. The day before she arrived had been spent in major preparation. I already knew I wanted no comments from family on how to integrate Julie into the family without slighting Steven…and no advice on what or how to cook or prepare formula. Normally advice flowed from the family like rain in a downspout.

Formula, of course, was the most important item they would want to discuss. In "the old days" of the 60s, preparing formula was a tiresome process: mixing the formula from the can, sanitizing the bottles in boiling water, pouring the nasty smelling creamy stuff into the bottles and steaming for what seemed endless hours, making sure not one germ survived.

In our case, it was a futile effort anyway. By the time Julie was six months old and crawling around, she was sucking on the piano pedals!

But at five pounds, when Julie came into my life, she of course was too tiny to eat the meatloaf with the hard boiled egg baked into the middle, or the pot roast with simmering tomato sauce and vegetables, or the must-have seemingly ritual chicken soup with rice carefully prepared with celery, carrots, parsnip and plump chicken.

I just knew that day I'd get a heaping of family advice. That was the first time I told everyone to get out of my life! Perhaps I did not want to follow the script any longer.

Julie now

17

When Cooking Wasn't Enough

Good or bad times, I cooked

Questions. What is it that compelled me to cook? Good or bad times, I cooked. Was it a sense of power that I can nurture and heal with my food? Or was it a sense of control over my life that I felt I did not have unless I was cooking? I couldn't blame this on Betty Crocker.

Tracking back over history, I realize now, cooking and hard times were intermingled. Many mothers were working back then. During Julie's teen years, I had a part-time job working for my brother-in-law Harry, selling, of course. He owned a linen store on the lower

East Side and I was able to be home when Steve and Julie got home from school. As I recall, it was Sundays at the store that were wild and crazy. All the linen stores in that area put out newspaper advertisements with discounts on their linens, drapes and towels. Our store was not far from Little Italy and many of the Mafia Mamas would come in then, especially when they needed items for their daughters soon to be married. I will never forget, when it came time for them to pay me, they would ask me to step into the back room where they would dig into their bosoms and pull out a baby sock filled with $100 bills.

I also will never forget one night a few years later rushing off to the emergency room in the middle of the night because Howard could not breathe. For two years he had been dying of cancer. I spent that night sleeping on a chair in his hospital room. We had moved to Denver a few years earlier because of his new job and the only family we had in Denver was Julie. I called her in the middle of the night to let her know we were at the hospital and that I would get back to her first thing in the morning.

Another question: Was his illness and later loss another nail in her coffin of depression?

In that hospital room, we were awakened at dawn by a nurse who flipped on the lights startling both of us out of our safe cocoon of sleep. Howard was now breathing normally. I could safely return home and tell the family all was well. For now.

Back home, after a hot bath, I went to the kitchen and put a chicken up to roast and made a pot of coffee. That simple act of cooking seemed to ground me, putting me back in charge and giving me some semblance of normalcy again. And Julie, now a grown woman, would soon be coming over and I wanted her to see and smell that all was well.

Cooking fragrances covered the smell of fear but could not dispel it.

Since her father's illness, Julie had been acting more strangely than ever. She cried more easily. She was so very quiet. She was so depressed thinking about the possibility of losing her father.

I think about my bouts with depression. Was all the cooking much more than I'd thought? Was it a cover-up to make times look and feel normal when the pressure of family life became too much?

———————

I continue to think about my funny, beautiful, chubby little Julie. Always the life of the party in her pretty plaid dresses with her curls, energy and ever-chatting conversation to anyone who would listen.

When did I lose sight of her? When did she begin to disappear into herself? Was I so busy making "Alice dinners," cooking her favorite foods, trying to please her and to show my love for her by cooking? And when family came over, was I doing the same thing then? Trying to please the whole family?

Was that the beginning of Julie's slide into depression? Was I there physically cooking but lacking an emotional connection? I recall so many years when, totally absorbed in making everything perfect for a family dinner, I would be unaware of my missing Julie. There was Steven and his cousins holding court and dominating all conversation with the adults. Precocious kids, the three of them. Bright and spoiled.

Later, when I would find her either in her own room or the spare bedroom at my mother-in-laws house, I would coax her to come downstairs and enjoy the special dinner I made for her and the family.

Unwillingly she would trudge along and join us at the table. While everyone was oohing and ahhhing over the food, the flowered dishes, the table decorations with the chocolate turkeys at each place, Julie would sit morosely at the table. It always made me uncomfortable pushing her to join in the conversation.

So here I am again, so many years later, cooking and writing this memoir and thinking about my Julie. What can I do to help her? How can I make her happy? And again I think: was it my fault she fell into this depression?

As I prepare a pot roast, onions, carrots, celery and potatoes browning in my Dutch oven, the fragrance reminds me how much Julie used to love pot roast. Does she still? I don't seem to know her any more.

———

Memories: I wonder if I was cooking when her first grade teacher called to tell me Julie was retarded and I should come in for a conference? I knew better. My Julie was far from retarded.

But I watched as she slowly slid away from me. As she grew older, she dropped her friends. She was cranky. She was no longer able to tolerate the people who loved her the most. She isolated herself from all of us. No delightful dessert or special Julie dinner would move her.

"I hate this feeling" she cried.

"Come into the kitchen and I'll make you a sandwich and a cup of coffee. You'll feel better."

Cooking and nurturing and trying to heal once again. But it was not working this time. No food would make her laugh or reach through the depths of her depression.

I continued to cook. For her, for me, for our sanity. We went to a therapist. "Any depression in her family?" she asked.

"Oh yes," I answered. "My mother…and me, a little." I fibbed to cover my own depression.

"Mom," Julie said, "You forgot I was adopted!" I had made light of my own depression because I did not want to upset Julie. But I truly did forget she was adopted.

When we went home, my heavy heart, smeared makeup and red eyes sent me to the bathroom to apply fresh makeup in order to face the world again. Makeup the cover up, just like cooking.

I asked her if she was hungry.

"A little" she replied.

I cooked her favorite Middle Eastern dishes. Stuffed squash with chopped meat and rice, leg of lamb, and rice with mushrooms and chickpeas. But she only had toast and tea.

She continued to slip away from all of us. No one could reach her. Not her therapist, not me, not her father and, it seemed, not even the medication.

When her father died, she plummeted out of control. Her crying was the sound of a whimpering wounded puppy. And that's just what she was. I was too exhausted after eighteen care-giving months to share my own grief or help her with her burden.

I continue cooking. For what, I think? I no longer have the need to make a place for myself in the family or find ways to bring us all together.

While cooking seems a powerful antidote to whatever ails you, it can't cure depression and it can't solve all the problems life throws at you. Maybe I'm selfish. Cooking comforts me.

———

Julie hit bottom with a thud shortly after her father passed away. "Mom," she said again, "I hate this feeling. I'm so tired. I feel like sleeping forever."

Thoughts of my mother taking too many pills with her brandy scared me. My mother recovered. I cooked for the whole family as she recuperated. I know they appreciated my cooking, but what problem did it solve? It only provided a venue for the family to sit around and discuss my mother's illness.

Julie checked into a behavioral health care clinic for a few days. Doctor's orders.

"What shall I bring you?" I asked.

"Just clean clothes, please," she answered.

"Would you like something to eat from home?"

"No food," she replied. It seemed like I had lost my power to heal, if I ever had it.

The first time Julie was released she came to my house. I tried to comfort her. But she could not stop crying, and for the first time I could not cook.

That's when I realized that my so-called power, cooking as healing, would not work, if it ever did at all. Julie checked herself into the center again several months later. When she checked out she went home. I called to see how she was doing and if there was anything she needed. "No thank you," was the reply.

I called again a few days later. "Come over and I'll make you your favorite dinner," I said, trying to recapture the healing power of food.

"I'm sorry, Mommy." A name I had not heard for many years. Through her tears she said, "I'm not home. I just checked myself in at the center. Can you bring me some clean clothes?"

I went to the kitchen once again. This time the cooking was to comfort me.

18

For Once You Have Tasted Flight

Learning to Fly Retractable Gear. Wheels up! Wheels Down!

Being present and in the moment. Something I never knew I could achieve until flying brought me to that moment. Kids, house, husband, wife of the 60s, always pre-occupied with something else. Except me.

Being one with the plane, as if I were poured into it. It encompassed all of me. The engines purring softly, the dials on the cockpit panel aligned perfectly. The sky above and the earth below.

Watching as the earth, like a green and brown patchwork quilt, slid by beneath me.

Feeling the sun through the cockpit window so warm on my body it felt like a lover's embrace. The peacefulness, knowing with all my heart that all was well in my small world.

Being alone, with just the crackle of the radio and the occasional voice of the controller checking in with me as I flew across Long Island Sound. Concentration so strong, it wiped everything else out of my mind. Just me and my plane.

Leonardo Da Vinci said, "For once you have tasted flight, you will walk the earth with your eyes turned skyward. For there you have been and there you long to return…"

Alice and Howard, Another Air Race

I couldn't describe it better. And Da Vinci never had the chance to slip a plane gently downward toward the runway. Nor, I dare say, had he watched the sun come up from a cockpit window lighting each cloud it touched like soft pink cotton candy. Indeed, it would be safe to say that he never flew a new and different plane just to see how it handled and what it could do. And he never had the opportunity or the pleasure to engage in "hangar talk," exchanging stories about the time my plane did this and I did that, hours and hours of boredom, punctuated by moments of panic.

"Remember..." my friend and flying partner Carol asked, "the time we thought we wouldn't clear the trees at the end of the runway?" Terror. "Remember when we flew the race and lost the airport?" Laughter.

Those moments of panic. A deal with God. Please God, let me get out of this safely and find my way home, and I promise I'll never fly again. Only to land and reserve the plane for tomorrow. One can only hope that God was not keeping count.

I owe these experiences to two men—my father and my husband. My dad said I could do anything I wanted to, even while the 1950s and 60s said I could not and should not. I should appreciate my life. What I have. The kids, the husband, the new dish washer. What turmoil it set up in my mind.

And Betty Friedan had arrived on the scene. What a ruckus she was causing in our tranquil domestic lives.

So, being a sort of rebel, I went out and learned to fly. Don't know why since I had lost two close friends to a nut who blew up their plane to get his mother-in-law's insurance. That was before the word terrorism became the word du jour.

Not so long ago, I actually had been afraid to fly in any plane, big or small. If it had wings, I wasn't interested. But Howard felt differently about flying. One day he came home and announced that next week we would both take our first flying lesson. Pretty unusual for a man in the 1960s. Most men would have said, "Be a good girl and get your hair done. I'm off to learn how to fly."

During the trial flight, my instructor swaggered out, promptly took the gum out of his mouth, glued it to the wing and announced, "There, that should hold it." He probably thought I would turn and run. But I simply reminded him that he too would join me if the plane went down.

As we trundled down the runway in a plane so small it could only hold two of us, something happened to me that was miraculous. I became a flying junkie! And, I soon learned how to swagger myself! I also discovered that I was highly competitive. On a clear sunny Saturday, my husband soloed. The next week I flew, as the saying goes, the doors off the hangar and soloed the following Saturday.

I was forty years old when I received my license. A much older gentleman at the airport, who had started out being very old after his wife had passed away and had become younger each week, said I had moxie! He knew the restorative power of learning how to fly and he understood the feeling of new life and new doors being opened to us!

Although I didn't know it at the time, that license changed my life. If I could do that what else could I do? It was the beginning of the end of the Betty Crocker era for me.

For there I have been and there I long to return. It was the only time I found myself in the moment. Completely in charge! Just me!

Richard Bach, the author of *Jonathan Livingston Seagull*, said, "The person who flies is responsible for their own destiny." I like that. Perhaps that was my reason to learn to fly. The meaning behind it all became quite clear: I was in charge of my life!

The spirit of Amelia Earhart and Charles Lindbergh accompany me. Just the three of us and the plane and the horizon.

19

Moxie

Next Up, Aerobatics!

Touch and go is a term used in flying, especially when learning. Land, touch the wheels on the runway, push the throttle to full power, pull the wheel back and rise up again to join the sky. Turn into the wind, capture the site of the runway, pull your throttle back to landing speed, and do it all over again. And again. And again.

One day my instructor jumped out of the right seat, just as I was ready to rumble down the runway for our next flight, patted me on the back and said, "Good luck, honey, you're on your own!"

My first solo! I couldn't wait for him to leave the plane! I had been expecting this to happen any day now. "The Husband" had soloed last week, I was chomping at the bit. I had to solo immediately to catch up! A bit of competition? More than that, I think.

I felt that I had to show the men, all of them, a woman can, will and did fly a plane as well as they did.

Now I was completely in charge of the plane, my life and perhaps my future. Joy!

Practice sessions followed and I struggled to keep up with the unfamiliar instruments. I was still lacking confidence when it came to calculations, computing the wind and speed, and hadn't overcome my aversion to mathematics. A sign of the times. Women should get married, stay home and have babies. Definitely not learn to fly!

Once it dawned on me that I was in charge, and all the work was something I had done over and over, I aced it. I was ready for my FAA written and flight test.

I thought that thirty-seven hours of flight time was way too long to earn your license. Until I heard that most people were not ready until fifty hours or more. It began to dawn on me that I was smarter than I thought!

After attending flight school two nights a week with Howard, it was time to go for my written exam, which I passed, and I was ready for the flight test. So happy that the bathroom at the airport was nearby as my stomach began to turn over. My palms were sweaty, I was a mess. *Focus*, I thought. *You have done all this before.*

The FAA appointed flight inspector swaggered over with a look that said, "Let's see if this little lady can fly a plane." I showed him! After an hour in the air, sweaty palms, churning stomach and all, I did it...

Later, license in hand, I swagger out to my beloved blue and white Cessna, number 550, to fly across Long Island Sound to Bridgeport, Connecticut, for the "$100 hamburger" as we called it. That was the cost of the fuel and the plane rental.

Before take-off I call the tower and ask for a water watch as I fly across Long Island Sound. A check-in every so often to make sure I have not fallen out of the sky and needed to be rescued.

Now it seems I am neither here nor there. Smack in the middle of Long Island Sound. My airport is behind me and Connecticut is in front of me. The engines are purring softly, the radio crackles, and I am alone snug as a bug in a cockpit.

To my left I can see the skyline of Manhattan, a rare clear day on the East Coast. I had done everything exactly as I was taught. Checked the weather and the winds aloft, did a pre-flight, which included checking the oil, kicking the tires, checking the instruments and buckling myself in. The smell of aviation fuel fills my nostrils as if it were perfume.

I look down and at three thousand feet, see the tiny sail boats, motor boats and the sparkling water. Peace.

The radio crackles. "550 How ya doin', Alice?"

I push the mike button and reply, "550 under control. Thanks."

"Great. See ya later, Alice."

My surprised voice asks, "How do you know who I am?"

Controller replies, "Alice, you always fly 550 and your name is on the flight plan."

"Oh, thanks," I reply.

Suddenly a gust of wind buffets my plane. My stomach lurches, I pull the throttle back a bit and descend to a lower altitude to see if the air might be calmer. It is. Stomach back in place. I fly on.

Once again I am accompanied by the voice of the controller.

"Uh, 550, you are coming up on the coast line. The airport is to your right. Dial 770 for Bridgeport Tower for landing instructions. Have a good day, Alice."

I contact Bridgeport tower. "This is Cessna 550. May I have the active runway?" A pilot must call ahead before entering the landing pattern when there is a control tower. Bridgeport responds, "Which runway would ya like, honey?"

I reply, "This is Cessna 550, cut the crap and give me the runway!"

Suddenly another voice takes over. "Cessna 550, this is Bridgeport tower, enter the pattern for runway 33 left. Call us on final approach. You are number three behind the Piper Cherokee. Have a good day."

I land, taxi to the parking area and, instead of going for my $100 hamburger, decide to go up to the tower to see the idiot who thought he was being cute.

Apparently he is on a break. My answer had stunned the tower, though. Apologies are in order and I receive one.

"Hey," I remind the guys in the tower, "this isn't a game."

Women were just becoming controllers about that time. Soon the voices of women in the control towers and in the FAA Flight Control Centers around the country were heard in the land! Answering women pilots both in commercial and private aviation.

Love it!

———

More stories…the year was 1969. I had just finished my first solo flight around the airport. Yippee! All I had to do was take my first cross country flight all by myself!

Cross country? So naïve, my first thought had been. "Who will watch the kids while I'm away?"

Cross country means one hundred miles or more, no New York to California trip. More like Providence, Rhode Island from our Long Island airport. Fly there, land, have your log book signed to prove you were there and fly home.

First I would need to use everything I had learned to plan the flight. Plot the course, plan the time, and gather information on winds aloft to be sure I would have the speed and fuel I'd need, then take the log book and file a flight plan. Was I nervous and excited? Both, I was taking this flight before my husband took his! That was nerve-wracking enough. Not that it was a race, of course, but then again, it did have all the earmarks of one!

Plotting the course required, as we called our map, a Sectional. A compilation of several states, in this case, New York, New Jersey, Connecticut, and Rhode Island-Boston. Listed were all the radio flight centers along the way. I jotted down all their numbers where I could easily find them.

My flight instructor and I went over the planned route and what the Providence, Rhode Island airport runways looked like, and how they were laid out to align with my compass and other instruments in my flight panel. I was ready!

I sauntered out to my blue and white Cessna 150, N number 550 to start my preflight check list. Remembering that I couldn't pull over to a cloud and call Triple A for directions while fueling the plane at the nearest cloud!

I buckled in and called the tower for takeoff instructions.

"Use runway 33, incoming traffic, hold your position," came the voice.

Then, "Clear for takeoff and good luck, Alice!" The boys in the tower knew me and my blue and white Cessna. Nice to have friends in high places.

As the song says, off I went into the wild blue yonder. I headed for the first compass heading after clearing the flight pattern of the airport.

Relaxing: all was well. The sun was shining, the engine was purring, the radio was crackling, and I was at peace. I checked my map and found the highlighted points along the way. I was right where I belonged.

Suddenly I looked down and saw Providence Airport! The runways were properly aligned, the time and fuel were right… Nah, I thought. That can't be right. I cannot and do not believe in myself that I did it right and I was there! It was too simple.

So I told myself to fly on. It can't be too much longer! I flew on and on. Suddenly I saw what looked like a major city in front of me. Boston! I called the FAA Center (whose radio number I always had available). Yes, they told me, I was in Boston controlled air space.

Nuts! I thought, that's Providence! But I said, "Thanks, I want to go to Providence Rhode Island Airport. Can you give me a heading?" They did and I turned the plane to that heading. Wishing I was a fly on the wall listening to their comments!

Now that it had been established between the Center and me that this was my first cross country solo, they start checking on me every few moments. "OK, I got it now," I told them after a bit. Away I flew!

Then I got switched to Providence tower. I was already overdue, according to my flight plan. The tower called my airport that I had their runway in sight and they had my plane in sight. I was still in the air and alive!

I asked Providence tower to give me the landing runway. They instructed me to follow my traffic, an Eastern Airlines commercial flight, and I'd be second to land behind them.

Suddenly I heard this wonderful male voice that sounded as if he was an announcer in his previous life, say, "Providence Tower, we defer to the little lady. Let her land first. We have been listening to her conversation with Boston Center and following her conversation with Providence Tower."

Well! Embarrassed, yes! Happy to land and have my flight log signed? Yes. Up in the tower, as I was having the log signed, I met the Eastern Airlines captain, who told me, for the second time in my life, "You, little lady, have moxie!"

I returned to my airport on Long Island to the applause of the people gathered around the control tower. The story of my flight had preceded me.

Alice and Carol, Air Race Completed!

View from my cockpit, preparing to land

The T-shirt says, "Will Fly for Food"

20

Too Soon Gone

Our Engagement Party, 1951
(L-R) Abe Borodkin, Mina Borodkin, Howard, Alice, Dad, Mama

Over the years there would be many successes but none quite as sweet as becoming a pilot and soloing. An accomplishment that had prepared me—more than anything else—for what lay ahead. Doing something truly on my own meant I could do it again…and again. Howard, part and parcel of my life since I moved next door at thirteen, was too soon gone from my life. Our first date had been at fifteen when he'd parked the car and tried to kiss me. And I told his mother. Now dead, from pancreatic cancer. We'd been married forty-seven years.

So began a new journey of self-discovery, tested and tempered like a piece of steel, which I found out later was so true. But unlike steel, underneath it all I was tender, caring and compassionate. Me.

Tested. They say that God never gives you more then you can handle. How I questioned that as I watched Howard struggle through the last months of his life, and the family along with him.

After that initial diagnosis we had sat grim-faced in the doctor's waiting room, like everyone else waiting to be called in once again to hear our options. We pretty much knew what we would hear and we had discussed what we would do, over and over. A very intimate decision it was: we would do nothing so that the last six months would be the best we ever had in our history.

Howard turned to me and said, "Isn't it too bad we had to come to this to get close again?" I knew what he meant. It made me sad to think of all the anger between us, the buried unspoken hurts, the growing pains of life. So we moved on…

Beautiful, warm sunny days when we needed to be together, just us, only we can handle the inevitable. We sit outside at the coffee shop, touched by the warm sun, mountains tipped with snow in front of us, so overwhelming, tears in my eyes. I'm scared, I'm not. I'm weak, I'm strong. I cannot see my life without him.

Like a sword his life dangles over his head. We seem to be mourning already. We speak of the past. The good things along the way, the bad things that stick like thorns and make us bleed, the funny things. Fifty years. My tears never cease. But the love that was stuck in his heart all came out during those last months.

We don't speak of the future now, not more than two or three months anyway. We plan a trip with our daughter Julie back to New York to see friends and family. Those family dinners now are quiet and subdued. Everyone seems to be walking on egg shells. Conversation is stilted. And here we are all thinking the same thing: This will probably be the last time Howard will come to New York. Perhaps the last time we will all sit around the table trying to make conversation.

Later, "Howard are you OK?" I ask.

"Allie, are you OK?" he answers.

I reach to hug him, my God, he is so thin and bony, but I say nothing.

Alice and Howard, Engagement Party, Memories Now, 1950

21

Lost in the Mist

Steven, Julie, Alice. Depression Kept Me from Smiling

Ⓗow can one describe depression? Deeper than sadness. Real gut-wrenching, deep, deep loss, a stone in the stomach, energy-sapping.

Waking each morning with that feeling of dread for another day. My companion, depression. How many of us really know those feelings?

Mama the Diva had it, but would not acknowledge it. Back then, no one did. So she drank her brandy, put on her makeup to hide the fear and saved her tears and anger for only us to see at home. I wonder if our shared DNA passed on those dark clouds shrouded in mist.

Or Dad. Happy, whistling bouncing-along Dad also suffered with his migraines as he tried to shoulder his families' problems and make everyone happy.

Did I inherit those dark clouds? Was it part of my DNA? Or did I succumb to it by the circumstances of my life? What caused me to slip into the mist and almost drift away? I wanted so much to drift away, to sleep in peace and stop feeling.

To some, my life read like a fairy tale. Accomplishments I never expected to achieve. But underneath the sadness of losing three babies through miscarriages and another through being born still and lifeless, I had been far enough along to learn that all of them were boys. I thought of them as my lost sons. Loss was my constant visitor.

This piled upon almost losing my life and my son Steven in childbirth. But at three pounds and with a strong will to live, he made it. And so did I.

And now Betty Friedan was calling it the Problem Without a Name. The feeling many young women felt in the 1950s and 60s and sometimes even today, of being unfulfilled.

Howard the boy next door who I married and stayed with forty-seven years through thick and thin. Howard. Creative, musical, an academic, should have been sharing his love of music on a college campus. Instead he was forced by the culture of the day to get a job, go into business and support his family. He too suffered from sadness and depression, I later realized. We were always struggling with financial insecurity and discontent.

Another nail in my coffin of depression.

Sapped of energy and tired of fighting life, nothing could lift the mist. Not my children, not my family. Nothing. Without thinking about it, I chose to end this cycle of pain and sadness.

Alone in our New York apartment one day, I headed to the bathroom where I emptied the entire cabinet of any and all pills that were there. I washed them all down with a bottle of Scotch.

I lay my head down to sleep forever.

What power or combination of the fates made me so sick I'll never know. Not long after, I headed to the bathroom once again and threw up the whole mess!

I slept. I awoke before Howard came home, took a shower and, shades of Mama the Diva, got dressed. Put my make up on. Set the table for dinner.

Did Howard notice the empty bottles in the bathroom cabinet? Did he see the empty bottle of Scotch? If he did he never mentioned it until so many years later.

Now I was angry. I simply could not stand myself or tolerate another day of this madness! I found a therapist. I knew without a doubt I needed help.

Howard had six months to live after forty-seven years of marriage. All pretenses dropped from both of us as we rounded that last corner.

"You know, Allie," he said, "I too cried when you lost those babies. And I often wondered about the pills and Scotch, but decided not to mention it."

"Imagine that," I replied.

I thought to myself, if only you had come forward then and said the things you say now, perhaps we could have avoided some of those years. I knew then that he had also been lost in the mist.

For me it was a wake-up call that I and only I was in charge of my life. It was the beginning of a new path. A new road to take that took some time for me to figure out.

Still today there is a bit of the cloud and mist of depression that follows me. But now I can wipe my eyes and move through the mist to live another fruitful day.

———

Writing a memoir unleashes such memories! I now recall how Mama, uncharacteristically perhaps, knowing I was suffering through depression at the miscarriages and a stillborn baby boy, would sweep into my house, plop my young son into the bathtub, open all the windows and blinds, make coffee and urge me to shower and dress. All in one breath! Then we would go out to lunch at a neighborhood luncheonette. I knew she knew how to deal with the blackness that surrounded me. She herself suffered from miscarriages and depression. But she never spoke about hers or mine. No words of sympathy were uttered.

You could say she bequeathed the depression to me, thankfully not the drinking. I surrendered to that depression until I figured out I hated feeling drained of energy and life…and I certainly did not need or want that kind of attention.

22

Women Who Broke All the Rules

Interviewing Pilots for My Newspaper, *Airport Press*

Book titles have always intrigued me. You can usually tell what the latest trend is by looking at the top-ten best sellers of the moment.

Lately they all seem along the lines of these fictitious titles: *Eat Your Way to Success* (or not), *Spiritual Fitness, How Women Can Win in the Stock Game* (my husband the expert says, buy low, sell high), *Feng Shui for Women* (so we chopped down a tree blocking the front door!).

And currently it's all about women who dare, care, broke all the rules, leaned forward, started over, overcame adversity, led balanced lives while looking like Cindy Crawford and cooking like Rachael Ray.

One of the books on my shelves is called *The Women Who Broke All the Rules*. It's an interesting title. Women of my generation had role models who never broke the rules! My mother-in-law, for example. She made breakfast every morning for her family, ironed her husbands' shorts and t-shirts, and turned out the best cooked meals for dinner. Dinner, by the way, was a family affair with everyone at the dinner table.

And then there was my mother, who ran our household with an iron fist, following all the rules. That's why we called her Diva!

Back then, we had books, of course, to guide us in our womanly duties, *The Good Wife Book, Ladies Home Journal,* and *Betty Crocker's Home Cooking.* They should have been titled, *How to Survive Marriage in Ten Easy Lessons.*

Life had its rules. Go to college, find a husband, get married, have a family and be a good girl! But it appears that I was one of those women who broke some of those rules. I felt ignored and like a second-class citizen. Yes, I got married, had a baby, cooked and cleaned, but I never felt I accomplished anything that used my college education or the things my dad taught me.

That's not to say there weren't extraordinary, not so ordinary women in those days. These brave individuals were forced to make choices and decisions that changed our political and social outlook forever. Representative Martha Griffiths, the first woman to serve on the House Ways and Means Committee, comes to mind. She was instrumental in getting the prohibition of sex discrimination added to the landmark Civil Rights Act of 1964. Griffiths is also known for resurrecting the Equal Rights Amendment (ERA). And there were many others.

I say forced to because, like me, many women felt like they were being ignored for who and what they were as individuals who had accomplishments of their own. We knew where we were, where we had been, but damned if we knew where we were going. Yet. And I wanted to be part of that change.

This goody-two-shoes was just dying to bust loose, beginning to feel squelched and stepped on. I remember the first rule I broke— just a few weeks after my wedding. In those days, polite young married women ordered engraved informal notes. Mine should have read: Mrs. Howard Borodkin. Mine said: Mrs. Alice Borodkin. When my mother-in-law questioned me about the name and asked if it was a mistake, I replied, "When I wear glasses, and grow a mustache I'll change it to Howard." Well! *That* had felt good!

She and I did go on to have a wonderful relationship for the next forty-seven years, once she began to understand who I was, which took forty-seven years.

I broke another rule right after my honeymoon by refusing to succumb to the move-over-honey syndrome on that rainy day. After all, I had a driver's license. My grandfather, the cab driver, had taught me to drive when I was thirteen! But it had taken guts to stand up for what I felt was right.

Thinking about that move-over-honey story makes me recall another story I wrote at the Kitchen Table Writing workshop, where I've been piecing together my life on paper…I called it, *The Road to Alice…*

Taking a journey, driving a highway, picking an exit, is this the right way? In the world of the 1950s not a lot of choices for the direction we should or would take.

We were locked into our roles, our direction already in front of us, the road laid out before us, the exit clearly marked. So little experience with life, how will I know which way to travel?

Taking the journey driving through life wondering if I made a wrong turn, took the wrong exit. Taking a journey. High road, low road, which one is right for me?

Along the highway of life we sometimes take a wrong turn, take the wrong exit, end up where we never thought or expected to be.

Taking a journey, getting lost, finding a new route, or do we continue down the same old road?

Taking a journey following an old map set up before time by those who came before me.

Taking a journey, finding a new map and a new exit called adventure, a road called experience, twisting and turning and yet the road goes on.

I see life as a highway, taking the wrong turn can be fatal, or wonderful, an unexpected turn can lead to disaster or the wonder of a new vista ahead.

I chose the road that seemed to be the right one for me at the time. Starting to meander towards marriage, children, home and hearth, security, safety, and the Feminine Mystique and Betty Friedan. My problem without a name.

Maybe I can make a U-turn and go back where I came from. Too late. The road is blocked. Keep driving. Where is the damn exit called me? The road to Alice?

So I keep driving, meandering down every road I find. Bumpy and un-paved, slick and asphalt covered. But still meandering. How do I get off this cloverleaf of exits, this roundabout of life?

The road goes on. And me along with it! I drive carefully!

23

Stop and Go!

From Good Wife to Radio Host, Denver, 1993

Simply put, I'd been brought up in a culture that said I could not do or be anything more than wife and mother. And that created such turmoil in my mind and my soul. Stop and go! Then along came Betty Friedan. Should I have been grateful? Now I was being pulled one way and then the other. Be a good housewife and mother! No, be true to yourself first!

So there I was, caught between the two Bettys. There was Betty Crocker, all smiles and domesticity, pulling me one way, and Betty Friedan, pulling another. Her book was such an eye-opener to women in those days:

Each suburban wife struggles with it alone. As she made the beds, shopped for groceries, matched slipcover material, ate peanut butter sandwiches with her children, chauffeured Cub Scouts and Brownies, lay beside her husband at night—she was afraid to ask even of herself the silent question—"Is this all?"

—from *The Feminine Mystique*

And here I was wondering, why not have both?

And, so, before those 60s came to a close, I was bucking the system all the time. I sought a part time job, I thought about going back to school, I dyed my hair blonde, I became an activist for women's rights and had groups of women come for coffee to discuss our issues. All this time Howard said nothing.

I came to realize that it's not so much what we wish for as it is a vision of what we want for ourselves in the future. For some of us from this generation, stumbling upon our success over a rocky road made reaching our vision all the sweeter.

My sister Ellen had a different vision for herself and I believe she has taken a similar path as mine but it has led in an entirely different direction. She too felt the stop and go.

I know where I came from through all the family stories, perhaps enhanced myths and family secrets told over and over again that seemed to have legs of their own, and handed down through both sides of the family. Most of those stories Ellen never heard. Ellen's story and her journey were tied to a different time and place. Each of us remember different stories at different times, and I don't remember some of the ones she has told me recently.

What ties us together? Completely different memories and life styles, exchanging our memories and stories now that we are older and wiser and can see them for what they are and how they affected us.

Both of us seeking comfort and support, each of us travelling on separate roads to fill our needs.

Ellen has her own story of growing up and I cannot tell it for her, only she can and has shared many moments with me. Many trials and tribulations of her own as Mama the Diva went down and down. Ellen got the brunt of that situation.

After I was married when Ellen was about eleven or twelve, we would meet for lunch or ice cream on a Saturday afternoon, just to spend some time together. I remember sitting at the ice cream counter one day waiting for her to join me when she came in looking tired and drawn.

"What's wrong?" I asked. With a gloomy "Nothing" from her turned down lips, I decided not to push on with questions. It seemed to me to be a normal day spent with my kid sister. We kissed and hugged goodbye and each went our separate ways toward home.

As I remember it, my husband was waiting for me with a message from my Dad. Mama the Diva had taken an overdose of pills. Ellen had known all along, but Dad had asked her not to say anything and she didn't.

Nor did she share the hard times of Mama's drinking, or Dad's business problems. Those problems I found out myself when we came to Mama's house for dinner. Arguments, screaming matches, tears were abundant. Fear and anxiety and drinking made Mama even worse than usual and harder to handle.

One day Mama drove our car into a brick wall. She said it was just an accident as the surgeon stitched up her chin. We all wondered about her excuse. We all thought it was another attempt at suicide.

To me my life felt like it was falling apart. To Ellen, it already had.

As she grew older and more beautiful, Ellen became engaged and married. Such excitement! I loved her so much and was so happy for her. I was still living in the days of Betty Crocker: Get married, have children, take care of your husband and home. I thought her married status would provide for her needs. I, of course, should have known better!

One day Ellen called me and asked, "I'm thinking about covering my head. What do you think?" Covering a married woman's head with a scarf or wig is an Orthodox Jewish tradition. Men must never be distracted from their study of Torah. Women's hair is considered a distraction.

Modesty is another part of the Orthodox Jewish culture. Necklines should cover your collar bone, long sleeves a must, and hemlines below the knee. However it doesn't preclude looking fashionable.

I loved the days when I'd visit and my nieces and sister would take me out for lunch, Kosher of course, and shopping in Brooklyn. Long sleeves and all.

As I think about it now I realize that she was discovering a community that would provide her with the comfort and security she had been seeking. Spiritually and physically.

"Fine with me," I replied. Whatever would make her happy made me happy. It never occurred to me that we would be at odds over this change of lifestyle. Actually I was happy for her, but surrounding me was my sister-in-law and her husband and the friends they both had in common.

I succumbed to their gossip about her life style. I was still in the mode of seeing myself through other people's eyes and still trying to be Alice the Good and Perfect.

The turning point in my relationship with Ellen came when she told me Steven could come to her home, but his wife, who was not Jewish, could not come. I felt obligated to make a choice and did so by choosing my son.

So started my downward spiral with my sister. We could no longer find common ground. We argued about everything. While I was seeking my own comfort and validation by choosing to pursue a career, Ellen had chosen Orthodox Judaism.

How ridiculous it all seemed to me! Dad had died, Mama was living in Brooklyn near Ellen, and all we had was each other!

I called her one day from Denver, where Howard and I had recently moved, and said I was coming to Brooklyn and wanted to talk. All I wanted was to sit in her kitchen and have coffee and talk. I needed comfort as well!

Slowly we began a new journey down the road to each other. Bumpy even now, but at least we can talk about it.

Ellen knows I respect her path to Judaism and the love it brings to her. All I ask is that she respects my choice to follow my own road to Judaism and the comfort it provides to me.

I adore Ellen and her family and her grandchildren. How I wish I lived closer to share all their life cycle events.

As we grow older, we seem to share the past more easily. Except my heart breaks when I hear her stories back then. And I'm sure I have not heard them all.

What a strange bond we have. But I hope it is tied up with love!

Dad and His Girls

24

Crashing Through

A Whole New Life at Sixty-six! Rep. Alice Borodkin

Those years during my marriage to Howard and before we'd moved to Denver when Howard got a job with RCA were marked by one effort after another to break out of the paper bag, like a frenzied cat, and go curl up on a ledge somewhere. But then I'd think, wait, I've soloed and earned a pilot's license. If I could do that, what couldn't I do?

More transitions…but I'd had to say goodbye to New York when Howard got that job. Off we went. I didn't mind. I knew it would lead to new paths, new careers.

Sure enough, not too long after arriving in Denver, I got involved in the women's and public relations communities after transferring my national memberships there. After a few years of holding various

PR positions, I founded the *Women's Business Chronicle*, a thirty-two page, all-business newspaper in Colorado. It had a circulation of ten thousand. It was my newspaper and, for the first time in my life, I was free to express myself without fear of being fired! Yelled at, nasty calls, and some overheated emails from readers, yes. But not fired. And since it was my paper, I even moved my editorial and picture to the front page when I started campaigning.

A few years later I gave in to that urge I'd be feeling for a long time. It was nice to be a newspaper publisher, but politics was beckoning and I responded. Again, just like with the *JFK Airport Press* that I'd founded, *Women's Business Chronicle* led me down a new path into politics. Seeing a huge need that I could help with, I ran for Colorado State Representative and won. Well, while I thought I knew about politics, it seemed I had a lot to learn! A little nervous in the beginning, I soon learned the ropes and to stand my ground.

There, I tried to control myself and be politically correct whenever possible. After all, this was 2001.

"Borodkin says it like it is! She always has an opinion."

I never quite knew what some lobbyists meant when they said, "Rep. Borodkin is so refreshing." Saying it like it is, is my way of facing the truth about those issues that affect us all, men and women.

Most of my time was spent on researching new legislation, which fortunately was available from organizations in Washington, D.C., and women's organizations whose lobbyists were eager and waiting for help with their causes. I felt confident and excited to go to work each day—working hard, doing it my way…but always mindful of the political process and structure.

I don't think anyone was surprised at my outspoken nature. It started with my campaign, when the man in charge of the House Majority Project called me and said, "We think you need to change your image. You are too New York City and too black with pearls."

"Really?" I replied. "Well, when you all become *Vogue* editors you can tell me how to dress!"

I stuck with who I was. Black with pearls and I won my seat four times!

I think, for me over my career, it was always a matter of being smarter than I thought. And I was always looking for more. More opportunity to pursue where it was I would fit in, trial and error, and then learning about how much I could do and how far I could go. Pushing the boundaries, they call it. Back in New York, when I'd begun my career, my first newspaper, The Airport Press, had been a significant learning experience. I had developed that newspaper while I was still flying regularly. To make a go of that publication, I'd started a Chamber of Commerce at JFK Airport to publish it. The motivation there was strictly to make The Airport Press the source for all news and advertising…and make more money.

What I find most interesting in those past newspaper columns I'd published is their relevance today. Either I was ahead of my time, not a good thing when one becomes a woman of a certain age, or we are still addressing the same issues. Perhaps, a bit of both.

I have to laugh now. I'd had absolutely no idea of how to produce a newspaper. The next best thing was to hire those who did. Of course this was all without money! I'd learned that lesson at age eight. Thanks, Daddy. So in exchange for their expertise, they were offered free advertising space for their businesses.

I'd gotten a reputation at the airport too. That had been because of my reporting on the mess in the off-airport cargo area. By publishing stories on the pot holes that swallowed up cars, zoning issues, driving too fast through the neighborhoods, homes built in the middle of all this, I'd created a political football. I was definitely getting a taste for speaking out. The JFK Chamber of Commerce, my creation, recently celebrated its fortieth anniversary.

Hurdle number one: I was a woman. At a Chamber board meeting I was expecting to be elected president. After all, the whole thing had been my idea. I wasn't. I didn't realize that I needed to advocate on my own behalf! The good old boy network had kicked in and a man became president. My ambition to be validated for who I was and what I did was not yet to be recognized.

It took some time until I realized that I could fight back politically—by starting the JFK International Women's Chamber of Commerce. To the surprise of the men, the Chamber flourished as women in business were eager to join and become active members of the community.

While social issues, such as getting the Port Authority of New York and New Jersey to develop a day care center for working parents of the airport, were discussed and acted upon, we were able to balance those issues with savvy business and political knowledge. That eventually led to political leadership and behind the scenes promotion of women in numerous areas.

Along the way, though, it was politics that got me revved. I saw firsthand that women were not being recognized for their worth. Could I change this? The hurdles I had to jump would be steep. I had been dealing with politicians who grudgingly recognized me as the publisher of Airport Press and perhaps as the founder of the JFK Chamber.

I was learning every day how to handle myself politically as I networked my way out of the Airport Press, and sold it to a man who thought he would take it nationally. I then took the job of Director of Marketing and Community Relations for the Metropolitan Airports Authority, an agency of the Metropolitan Transportation

Authority. But I also was getting the usual remarks about who was home cooking and taking care of the kids, and some unexpected offers to go to bed from men who thought I would be honored and thrilled at the invitation.

Since we owned two airports in New York State, I got to fly myself to work each day between airports. And, while I was the only woman on management staff at the Airport Authority, I was never treated as anything other than a member of the professional staff. I delivered a no-nonsense management style and professionalism. Imagine having so much fun in a job and getting paid for it—and being treated as an equal. But why shouldn't it be so?

So, what about the Bettys? How did these two clashing ideals affect me and most women's lives during those years after *The Feminine Mystique* came out? Although I can't speak for other women, I believe my feelings were very similar to most. In a way, it had been like getting a death-sentence reprieve when we were told we didn't have to make a career of being a housewife and mother. We could be more. Many women had gotten a taste of what it could be like during World War II, when we were running the country while the men were away. At my house, it was my father who had opened the door to equality by teaching me what he knew and giving me the chance to use those skills. But, and here's the bigger issue, while it may have seemed like a reprieve, we had to figure out how to morph into this new, liberated person. We also had strong opponents telling us how wonderful the old ways were!

Did Betty Crocker's minions (the happy stay at home moms, the housewives, our moms) ever help guide us as we tried to circumnavigate what Friedan was telling us was the Problem Without a Name?

Not really. Was the solution buried at the back of that Good Wives' book? Could we clean the house, serve our spouses their meals and then tell them, "Be back at 9, dear. I have an important meeting to attend. Oh, and please make sure the kids brush their teeth before bed"?

Was the solution instead found at the beginning of *The Feminine Mystique*? "It is no longer possible to ignore that voice," Friedan wrote, "to dismiss the desperation of so many American women. This is not what being a woman means, no matter what the experts say. For human suffering there is a reason; perhaps the reason has not been found because the right questions have not been asked, or pressed far enough. I do not accept the answer that there is no problem because American women have luxuries that women in other times and lands never dreamed of; part of the strange newness of the problem is that it cannot be understood in terms of the age-old material problems of man: poverty, sickness, hunger, cold. The women who suffer this problem have a hunger that food cannot fill."

Did we indeed have to reinvent ourselves?

Some of us were already primed for this. We *had* been doing it our way…walking the tightrope, playing it within the rules, learning the fine art of negotiating, reading between the lines of what was said. The looks we got when we did speak out, most often to family, gave us great feedback. We learned how to be two-faced. We employed the quiet way of using the Betty Crocker method of preparing a good meal, kissing Mr. Wonderful when he arrived home and then waiting until we saw the perfect moment to pounce! Well, okay, maybe not pounce, but to articulate what we wanted or needed. And, aside from my move-over-honey-I'll-drive fiasco, I did know how to temper my Betty Friedan side.

Interestingly, politicians use this method today. Watch and wait and read people and look behind the scenes for the answer on how to proceed. I think most women have that sense today. We seem to know what is really being said or done. Now we call it educated intuition.

I had a mentor and boss while working at the Airport Authority who, after a meeting, would always call me into his office.

"OK, Alice," he would say, "Now tell me what you *really* saw and heard. You women always seem to see and hear what we men do not!"

Patronizing? Absolutely not. He was always a strong proponent of women's rights. And he was right about women's intuition!

Women's Business Chronicle

25

Look, They're Tilting

Arnie and Alice's Wedding

When we were very young all our stories started with "once upon a time" and ended with "they lived happily ever after." But the stories left out the center. Sort of like a roast beef sandwich without the meat.

What about the meat, the center of our lives? What happens to us as we strive for the happily ever after? Is there a happily ever after and, if so, what are we doing to prepare for it?

Yes, I entered a new stage in my life when my first husband passed away. Now I was a mother, sister, sister-in-law, aunt, grandmother and a widow.

I have been called remarkable for the way I handled Howard's illness and his passing: how prepared I was, how in such a short time I'd been able to carry on. I am not remarkable. Albert Einstein was remarkable. I learned what to do and how to do it. I learned how to keep the meat in my sandwich. I learned how to prepare.

And that's the secret for all of us.

Running a business taught me to seek out the best. The best accountant, the best lawyer, the best financial advisor, the best book-keeper. It taught me to seek advice and to trust their judgment and mine to grow a healthy business.

So I applied the same train of thought to my new role, before it became my new role.

True, I had a warning about what was to come and the word denial was and is simply not in my vocabulary. Whatever it is you are facing, business or otherwise, face it and prepare. When business is good or life is good we tend to coast. That is the time to seek out those people we trust who help us prepare for happily ever after.

I have said many times that entrepreneurs need not feel alone in their struggles. There are plenty of support systems in place for us. We must be open to them and trust their advice as well as our own gut feelings and intuition. The same applies in our personal lives.

Many people, both men and women, abdicate their role in a relationship or business to someone else. It's easier to let someone else do the books, balance the checkbook, take care of the insurance, make the decisions that will affect our happily ever after.

Our happily ever after depends upon our knowing and taking charge of our lives in good times and bad. Whether it's business, a divorce or a death, know where you are at all times. Set goals. Plan ahead.

If you see your business or life is going sour, start planning. What are your options? Whom do you need to contact for advice? Financial planning is a critical part of life, but it's not the only piece of the puzzle. We need legal advice, spiritual guidance, banking knowledge. And it doesn't hurt to have good psychological counseling to keep us on track and to make sure we don't miss the forest for the trees. Those therapists may show us the way to not make the same mistakes over and over again.

As they used to say in the old TV program, *Hill Street Blues,* "Take care of yourself, it's cold out there."

Absolutely! But you don't have to do it alone to keep happily ever after a part of the meat in your sandwich of life after once upon a time...

After Howard died, the last thing on my mind was meeting a man and getting married again. After all, how many men were standing in line to meet a sixty-five-year-old widow without money?

Life at that time was a bit out of kilter for me, like an attached umbilical cord that set me floating in space. No anchor at all, just free floating in space...no sense of time or place, no schedule to follow.

Out of the blue a phone call from a friend: "So how do you feel about meeting someone now?" she asked. It had been a few months.

"Uh," I stuttered, "I don't know, the last time I had a date was fifty years ago." I could hear her husband in the background shouting, "For God's sake, leave the woman alone, the body is still warm!"

"Be quiet!" she yelled back.

I felt I should show interest. "Who is he?" I asked, not really caring at all about who, what or anything about him.

"His name is Arnold and he just lost his wife," she replied using her match-making voice.

"OK," I said in my I'm doing you a favor voice. "I'll see you at your party." I could check him out in a crowd and leave if I didn't like what I saw, I thought. So what was I thinking then, trying on clothes, then taking them off, then starting over until I found the right outfit?

The unconnected feeling continued as I drove through ice and snow to the holiday party. The road was dark. I started to cry. This is not for me! I need to go home to my safe, warm house, my dog and my wine. I'm too old for this crap!

Suddenly I found myself parking in my friend's already crowded driveway. Which car was his? Who cares? Still, as if in a trance, I walked though the open door, greeted and accepted condolences from mutual friends, as I headed to the bar. What the hell? I thought. If I can't drive home, I'll sleep here tonight and go back in the morning.

Without warning, the door bell rang and as my friend opened it, she said, "Hi Arnie, come on in and I'll find Alice."

"Oh, that's him," my disconnected brain said. "Nice-looking man." We were introduced eventually as I checked him out and listened in on his conversation with the people he knew.

We spent the rest of the evening talking over wine and coffee, speaking about our departed spouses, our adult kids, what he did, what I did, and how disconnected we both felt since the death of our spouses.

Arnie flew to London the next day to visit his daughter and grandchildren, and I spent Sunday with *The New York Times*, my beloved dog and a large glass of wine.

As New Year's Eve approached, the first one without Howard since I was fifteen, I can't believe my chutzpah, I called him and asked if he wanted to join a group of women friends… the rose among the thorns, I'd said…for a movie and dinner out. Oh! He said yes!

Time went on. We had dinner a few times, he asked for a hug, I panicked and shut the car door on his hand! He met my therapist, I met his, and all were in agreement that we should continue dating. But how, I thought? I'm sixty-five!

So I invited him to Friday night services at our synagogue. What could possibly happen there, I thought? But our emotions seemed to be growing into a fondness for each other. I trusted him. Did I love him?

Later a friend who had been sitting in back of us at the synagogue told me, "I poked my husband and whispered, 'Look, they're tilting.'"

That we were. Tilting toward love and joy that we had been blessed to meet each other.

We were married and are living happily ever after!

———————

So I started my whole new life at 66, and that's when I ran for office and won!

Alice and Arnie on the Rubber Chicken Circuit

26

Working for Good

Honorable Alice Borodkin and Representative Paul Rosenthal.
Presentation of Resolution for Legislation Concerning Women's Rights

O f course that was not exactly a straight course to the legislature. First I had to move to Denver and start all over again at age fifty-five. Then there was my time as publisher of *Women's Business Chronicle*, when I discovered how women entrepreneurs, after so many years, were still having problems starting their own businesses. As publisher I had a platform to share my feelings about this issue. As a result the Small Business Administration awarded me the Media Person of the Year for Region 8.

What drove me to the legislature were the women. Feeling their pain and their longing, I wanted to see women move forward and it was the one reason I chose to run for office. But, as it turned out, there were even more pressing issues facing women than simply equality with men, not only in Colorado but around the world. Addressing those issues became part of my platform.

I couldn't fix the world, so for the time being I concentrated on those issues at hand in my state—domestic violence, the wage gap, women's health and reproductive rights, sex and age discrimination, and human trafficking.

Then, as a member of the House of Representatives, I was given a scholarship by the Center for Women Policy Studies and the Foreign Policy Institute to attend some meetings in Washington, DC and later five days at the United Nations at a workshop/conference. The topic? Women, Peace and Security.

It was there that I learned about UN Security Council Resolution 1325, and the effort to bring more women into the peacemaking process. 1325 was a landmark international legal framework addressing the impact of war on women, and also the role women should and do play in conflict management, resolution, and sustainable peace. It had been introduced in 2000 and hardly any countries had signed on by the time we got there in 2004. Then, in December 2011, President Barack Obama released the first ever U.S. National Action Plan on Women, Peace and Security (NAP) as an Executive Order.

But Executive Orders can be overturned by the next administration. In order to put that National Action Plan into legislation, on July 13, 2013, The Women, Peace and Security Act (H. R. 2874) was introduced in the U.S. House of Representatives. This should ensure that the United States would continue to implement women's involvement and participation in the peace process.

Returning to Denver from that United Nations workshop, my head was full of thoughts on the global issues of women. So it was quite a distressing blow to learn that right under my nose, in our very own neighborhoods, in fact, human trafficking was going on as well. That's when I noticed a new spa had opened next door to a frequently visited restaurant on a busy highway right in Denver.

Oh good, I thought, *how convenient to have this in my own back yard!*

The very next day newspapers all over Colorado described the sting operation that closed at least sixteen spas in Denver, all with women and girls trafficked from Asia.

The kicker: my newly found spa was one of those closed, along with two others also in my House District. I quickly learned that human trafficking not only crossed the border of Colorado, but crossed right over into my own neighborhood.

Being an elected official, I thought, why couldn't I fight this scourge to human rights? I quickly contacted my colleagues from the Foreign Policy Institute who had already started working on the issue in their states. I knew that the states of Florida and Washington had already passed legislation to create a task force to study the issue of trafficking. That, I thought, was the way to introduce the issue in Colorado. When you are a legislator, you learn that there is no subject under the sun that does not have a piece of legislation already in place. So with that in mind, I sent for copies of Florida's and Washington's legislation and got the ball rolling.

And that's how House Bill 1143 became the Inter-Agency Task Force on Human Trafficking. Primary sponsor: Representative Alice Borodkin. I was doing something important at last.

For women who have awakened to new possibilities in middle age, or who were born into the current women's movement and have escaped the usual rhythms of the once traditional female existence, the last third of life is likely to require new attitudes and new courage.
—Carolyn Heilbrun, *Writing a Woman's Life*

Governor Bill Owens, Representative Alice Borodkin.
My first bill signing!

27

My New Moniker

Look Who Is Holding *My* Award!
My Boss at Metropolitan Transportation Authority, New York
and Alice, Director of Marketing for MTA, 1982

As a woman of a certain age, been there done that, I have earned a place in society, hard won to be sure. What I really want to say is…women, we are not done with our fight yet.

Betty Friedan in her later book, *The Second Stage*, wrote, "The uneasy sense of battles won, only to be fought over again, of battles that should have been won, according to all the rules, and yet are not, of battles that suddenly one does not really want to win, and the weariness of battle altogether, how many women feel it?"

And like Betty Friedan, I went on to my second stage and now the third stage. And just as her quote said it all, I felt the battle for my rights as a woman and a human being made me tired, but made me stronger, and has pushed me into the New Feminism.

I do not have to take sides as Friedan said in *The Feminine Mystique*. I do not have to be strident in my approach to having it all. In fact I do have it all.

Caught as I was between the Bettys helped me see that I can cook and clean and love my family and plant flowers in pots and still be me. Political and continuing to fight for the rights we fought so hard to gain in the first wave of the feminist movement.

———

Looking back, I see that growing up in the 1940s and 50s, about the same time as Friedan, Steinem and Abzug, and facing the wave of culture change from one Betty to another, we forgot we were getting older. Who thought about getting older? It seems everyone but me thought about age. I was turning 40 and then 41 and then the next thing I knew I was 50.

But I pushed on. My age never stopped me nor did I ever consider that I was old, until one day after I was hired by the NYC Office of Economic Development. Again connections helped as the director was a personal friend of mine. But again, I was prepared to make this my new career.

Stepping into the office for my first day, I was greeted by my friend, the director, with "Good morning, Alice, don't worry about being the oldest in the office and don't let your age interfere with your work. Welcome."

My age? I was just 48 or 49 at the time. I did get a late start on a career, I know, receiving my pilot's license when I had turned 40. But I was far from ready for a nursing home! In fact I had just left the MTA as a director of marketing.

In that job, I had been given the multi-million-dollar marketing of the Train to the Plane, the JFK Express. I prefer now to say I earned it. This partly because I understood airports, and partly because my boss at the Airport Authority went to bat for me. I was ready to step up to the plate either way.

In that position, I met with our advertising agency, sent our research staff out to JFK Airport to see who our market was, and decided how best to reach that market. What we found was that foreign travelers were more prone to using public transportation than US citizens were. I still have the story boards and copies of the campaign.

We created an award winning multi-language campaign designed to reach this market. As we were going in to make the advertising presentation to the representatives of the governors of New York and New Jersey, my boss turned to me and said, "You keep your mouth shut!"

I could feel the tears welling up and the hot flush creeping up my neck to my face. I did keep my mouth shut. Betty Crocker and the culture of the 1950s kicked in as I did what I was told.

I was not fired from the MTA because I was old. My whole department was fired as they decided to decentralize marketing to each individual agency. Furious once again, I packed up all my agency's marketing plans so that anyone taking over would not once again steal my trophy!

Gloria Steinem is younger than I am by one year. I recently read about her in *The New York Times* (as she was interviewed by Gail Collins, author of *When Everything Changed*). The article was titled "This Is What Eighty Looks Like." I was thrilled to get validation that some of us have crossed over at that age to being ageless and are now regarded as wise women. Women who, it seems, have weathered the storm of change and are now to be respected, listened to and admired. I like my new moniker.

28

Advocating for Me

I Won!

Today I am a recovering politician and the founder and organizer of Women Engaging Globally, a 150-member organization working on issues that concern all women. Human rights issues as Hillary Clinton said: "Women's rights are human rights!"

I often laugh when people ask me, "How long were you in for?" Sounds like a prison sentence. While it was far from being in prison, there were times it felt like it. The Legislature has its rules and process and the politics often cloud the issue. But experience taught me to challenge the system, and look behind and beyond the politics.

Truth be told, I loved that job! At last all the experience I had garnered over a lifetime came into play. After all, my dad had taught me to be an expert salesperson.

So selling my legislation to a committee of skeptics, and the Speaker of the House, was a piece of cake! And campaigning meant selling me and what I would do for constituents when I won that seat to represent them.

It was not easy as a woman, and harder still as an older woman of sixty-six, to get the attention of the younger men who strutted around and fancied themselves the next President of the United States!

It was even harder still the first four years being in the Democratic minority in a conservative state, coming from New York City as a liberal Democrat! What had I gotten myself into this time?

Someday my fellow legislators and I will write a funny book called Stories from the Campaign Trail! My favorite story for the book would be: In campaign mode, as I knocked on a door one day, a young man opened it and we started chatting. Then he said, "Oh, I would love to vote for you, Alice, if I could!"

"Are you not registered? I have a registration form right here." I asked.

"No," he replied. "I'm a felon."

So we started a "Felons for Alice Committee"!

―――――――

With so many challenges ahead of me, I always thought I could and would make a difference by the legislation I carried and had passed into law.

Human rights, the first person to pass a Bill concerning Human Trafficking. Animal Cruelty became a felony. Tourism and the arts became part of economic development. And I crossed the aisle to get what I needed and wanted.

Not unusual for women. It's the way we work! Collaboratively!

———

Colorado has term limits for elected officials, so after eight years, I found myself out the door with all my legislative experience. Not completely though. My passion for human rights and women's rights led me to chair a few women's organization boards, lobby for those issues I believe in and teach advocacy and the legislative process.

In this second stage of feminism, as Friedan has called it, or as I call it, the re-invention of Alice again, I have been fortunate to use my organizing skills and leadership roles and Dad's street smarts once again in pursuing my passion for the empowerment of women. Women globally and women right here in our United States. I know about empowerment!

I must give credit to one of my co-writers in our writer's group.

"Alice," she said, "You need to start an organization with all the experience you have on women's issues."

And that's how Women Engaging Globally began. Our goal is to become, through our coalition partners and members, the ultimate authority on global women's issues. It began as a grassroots effort and quickly grew to more than 150 members. I am inspired by the women and men who have rallied and jumped in to make this all happen.

It is experiences like this that I want to share with the young women of today. Learn from the past so you don't make the same mistakes we of my generation did. You can make a difference! Don't be afraid to challenge the system, ask questions and always cross the aisle!

———

I recently read a poem by William Wordsworth: "The World Is Too Much With Us." Indeed it is. Social networking has brought us untold immediate communication. I'm sure that many things we read instantly about, at the same time they are happening, were happening when I was a kid as well. In our innocence we didn't know about the issues. In our innocence we were immune to the struggles of the universe.

One thing I learned from the Bettys was that without thinking about it, I used the political intuition and the skills many women have, which are familiar to us all. Perhaps they are innate. How to negotiate around the agendas of family and friends that did not "get it" as I grew out of my cocoon of the 1950s. How to get what I wanted in the work environment.

It never occurred to me that I was part of the "Women's Lib" feminist movement of the 1960s and 70s. Even though I marched down 5th Ave. with the likes of Gloria Steinem, Betty Friedan and Bella Abzug, I'm not sure I knew why. Except it was all about me once again bucking the system! And the "equal rights part" sounded right to me!

At that march, I looked around and wondered if it was the right venue for me. I thought I had wanted something for women, but wasn't sure this was the way to get it. A bit too strident, I thought.

With Betty Crocker watching over my shoulder and Mama the Diva clinging to my psyche, I asked, "What am I doing being surrounded by these chanting women, placards held high, loudly demanding the Equal Rights Amendment be passed?" I kept marching, but I was silent.

In those days, women's libbers were sometimes profiled as lesbians, I was not; never shaved their legs or armpits, I did; never took a bath, I did; wore no makeup, I did; and donned beatnik clothes, I didn't.

Just the other day, I received an email from a colleague asking if I was going to DC to march for the ERA this year.

"Are you kidding me?" I'd asked. "I already did that—forty years ago."

Today there are millions of women who take equality for granted. Don't, I tell my audiences and bloggers, no matter what you call yourself, feminist or not—what we have gained in the past can be lost if we don't keep that fire ignited!

———

So what did I expect? What did I want?

Flash forward. After that march, I am walking, not marching, down the hall of the Colorado State Capitol, with another group of strong women—this time tough legislators. And I am one of them!

We chatted as we walked towards the House floor about forthcoming legislation concerning women—from reproductive rights to health care for everyone, Social Security, abused children and foster care in Colorado. And of course about our home life, husbands and boy friends or girlfriends who supported our work.

Mind you, these were Democratic women and Republican women! We were women first and all concerned about the issues facing us. Sometimes we even agreed! But we knew we had to work together if we wanted progress.

Our ages ranged from 25-66 and older. Some of us remembered the old days and the beginning of the feminist movement. Most of us needed to tell the younger women what and how we worked to get where we were now!

Colorado now has so many women legislators there was a line outside the women's restroom!

Like me, some of us had a past—as domestic feminists—and we had battled our way quietly through the 1950s and seem to be doing it still and again.

As a famous ball player said, "It ain't over 'til it's over!"

Unfortunately there were more than a few whose husbands I never met during my eight years in the House. Apparently these men wanted nothing to do with their wives' careers in politics. I think they were in the minority, however. One of my colleagues' husbands had badges made up for some of the men (mine included) for an organization called H.O.W.L. Husbands of Women Legislators. No meetings, no organization, just supporters of their wives in the legislature.

———

Did I have a college degree? I went to The Fashion Institute in New York for two years, and got repeat training on how to be like Mama the Diva. I learned how to put on fashion shows and became the fashion editor for the school magazine. Always missing deadlines for the magazine, I ended up writing an editorial on a paper napkin as I ate my lunch and handed that to the dean. Who, by the way, would stand at the elevator door every morning making sure we all were wearing our hats and gloves.

After graduation I went on to Queens College to get my Married with Children degree. Graduation was on Thursday and I got married on Sunday. Ready to use my M.R.S. degree!

But the school of hard knocks was the best college I ever went to (thanks, Mama), and the lessons and street smarts of my dad added the perfect touch to my education. Mama's lessons in culture and being a diva didn't hurt either. Once I figured out how to combine all these traits and lessons and apply them to whatever I was going to do, I became more confident.

But confidence took a long time in coming. That old Betty Crocker attitude and the culture of thinking *I'm just a woman and not too smart* was very hard to overcome.

How did it all come together to form the real Alice? How did I transform from a sort of privileged child into a competent woman, encountering adversity, getting smarter and gaining courage?

The whole time I was climbing the ladder to me, I learned how to advocate for myself. In doing so I was unwittingly at first advocating for all women and unknowingly setting myself up as a leader, not a victim. I like this Alice.

I have just finished reading *When Everything Changed*. It clearly shows the strength and power we have by saying, "Hey! Look at me! This is what I want or don't want." Too many of us have become apathetic and are letting the other guy do it. Actually allowing someone else to think for us. But let something slip by and become law? Most of us are shocked. "How did that happen?"

So it seems, after having served eight years in the legislature, and watching bills go by without a peep from anyone, that we need to change. Talk must turn to action.

Advocacy is not hard if you feel passionate about human rights. If you feel passionate about equal pay for equal work, if you feel that human trafficking is an insult to humanity, if women dying by the thousands in childbirth around the world disturbs you.

Teaching Flying to a Group of Students in Jamaica, Queens, New York.
Keeping Kids in School!

29

Circles of Life

Julie and Steven

These days I cook just for the joy of it. No more following the script written by generations of wives and mothers before me. I do it because I want to, not because I should.

Today, with my political career behind me, I fill my home with the luscious smells of allspice, cumin and cinnamon—and enjoy every bit of it. Did you know that real estate agents advise home sellers to bake cookies with cinnamon when showing a house? It seems their warm and welcoming scent make for an easier sell.

After we got married, when Arnold and I stepped into the house we hoped to buy, the bright sunny kitchen beckoned to me. I knew immediately that this was home. All I could think of was that I wanted to fill this home with the smell of good old-fashioned cooking. Arnold had gone directly to the basement where the furnace beckoned to him!

Food preparation, like making a bed or gardening, allows me the opportunity to work physically while my mind wanders between today and yesterday. Now my bookshelves also reflect my new life. Cookbooks—hello, Betty Crocker!—and files full of recipes. I have a kitchen stocked with the proper knives, blending machines, and hard imported cheeses to use with my new imported grater. Not to impress or be perfect, just to enjoy the pleasure of cooking. The house filled with the fragrance of roast beef with cumin and allspice brings me comfort and joy and a sense of pride.

Back then, the table had to be perfect, as I followed the script and the book because I had to rather than wanted to. Steven had to be perfect. Julie had to be perfect. The whole dinner became an event that needed to produce harmony whether it was a family gathering or a friendly social dinner with friends.

Perfection, planning, harmony, and control of the situation at hand. I see now. Not such a bad life after all. Thank you, Mama the Diva. I miss you.

These days Julie occupies my thoughts. My daughter and friend Julie. That's what she has become today at fifty-two. I believe part of her depression over the years has been due to the loss of her Grandpa Moe, her dad and now, in a way, even her brother. No, Steven is not dead, just missing in our family life.

The drama he has caused by ignoring me and his sister has left a hole in both our hearts. But both Julie and I are strong and have moved on with our lives.

Julie knows me. Julie knows my Betty Crocker ways of cleaning the house and the office. Keeping everything neat and in its place.

When I started *Women's Business Chronicle*, Julie's depression was severe. However she still would come to work in my office and she was good at keeping things running for me. She also knew that she was safe and could share her bad days with me and even take some time off. I often wondered if I was too protective or enabling. I guess all mothers do.

Yet, as Howard became sicker and weaker, Julie seemed to become stronger and would leave the office to stay home and take care of her father. In fact, I discovered that God works in strange ways. Not only did she take care of her father, but that allowed me to work full time at the paper.

But, as Howard began failing, others appeared in my life as I had to be out of the office more and more. People seemed to know what I needed. And then, after he passed and I went back to work people in advertising sales, editors, writers…all appeared and then disappeared after Howard's funeral when I went back to work.

Those were hard times for Julie. And for me as well. Somehow we survived with lots of help from our wonderful therapists.

After winning my election to the Colorado House of Representatives, Julie became my legislative aide. I don't know if I could have managed as well without her. As I said, she knows me well! She organized the whole office and me along with it. Files were up to date, messages answered, calendar perfect—and she handled herself like a pro.

But there were some difficult days. Days of crying, and sleeping too much and eating alone on her couch at home. Her weight climbed and with it her blood pressure and cholesterol. Finally she decide to have weight-loss surgery. I believe that and my being more emotionally there for her have helped her through. Today she is eighty pounds lighter, better able to cope with issues that once brought her down, and is becoming more independent with each passing day. But we both understand that black cloud of depression that hovers over both of us can still cause some rain.

I am so grateful that fate brought us together and that we have become more than mother and daughter. We are best friends.

Whatever you choose, however many roads you travel,
I hope that you choose not to be a lady. I hope you will
find some way to break the rules and make a little trouble
out there. And I hope that you will choose to make
some of that trouble on behalf of women.
—Nora Ephron, Commencement Address,
Wellesley College, 1996

30

What I Really Want to Say...

My Turn— Your Turn

Recently someone asked me how do you want your book to end? I don't know about the book, but I'm damned sure I don't want anything in my life to end!

Writing this book created something I never expected. A personal journey. My journey, my life experiences, my regrets, as Frank Sinatra sang, "I have a few," my potholes of life.

Now I see a new source for new beginnings. New beginnings can be and have been happening to me all my life. Even at the wise old age of eighty-one. Now I see what all the stories of my life add up to.

The author Joan Didion wrote, "We tell ourselves stories in order to live." Stories make the fabric of our lives. My stories make me who I am today. And it seems I am still creating them as I move through life.

It never occurred to me as I first sat down to write these stories about my life that I might be telling the tales of my generation and what women have been through over the years in the fight for equality.

And it definitely did not occur to me that telling my story might enable the young women of today to put their lives in context as they could see the transformation I went through and continue to evolve even today. I became a pioneer it seems who took on impossible battles to attain my goals. Those battles continue as women battle for equal rights and human rights.

I still find it hard to believe that I earned a pilot's license. That was a battle with my self-confidence. Gee. Little me, flying a plane? Look what that started!

And marching down 5th Ave. in New York City in the early 1970s to protest inequality? Another battle fighting the culture that wanted to keep women down.

How about starting a newspaper at JFK Airport? And two chambers of commerce? I hardly knew what a chamber of commerce was or did. And I knew nothing about publishing a newspaper. All of these were my challenges to prove myself and to become an independent woman in a "man's world."

Today I still battle on to help women become equal and independent. Only now I see it becoming a woman's world that we want to be in. And in that world we are validated for what we contribute and who we are. I too have moved on to my second and third and maybe fourth stage. What have I really learned? I never had to choose one Betty or the other. I can be me. I can cook and clean and plant my flowers and still be the political activist I was meant to be.

Because remembering what it was really like, what it was to live in a time in the 1940s, 50s and 60s, and how I fought the system to become who I am today allows me the privilege of hindsight.

Although I fought against the rules of the day, I was not a radical feminist, I did not neglect my femininity and I did not participate in the sometimes radical and shocking behavior of my female counterparts.

Indeed a bit of Betty Crocker has remained. But I certainly did follow the Friedan train of thought! I certainly did follow every move of Gloria Steinem and every issue she fought for.

I also learned that I had a big mouth and people were listening to me. What I did not learn was that many members of my own family did not hear me. Perhaps they were the catalyst way back when that set my path to proving who I was and what I was made of.

―――――――

Another piece to the puzzle of who I am, when I think of all my roles: mother, of course is a huge part of the story. And my story would not be complete without sharing this letter I wrote in my mind and never sent to my son, who I haven't seen in years:

To Steven:

"Where were you when I was acting out?" you'd said.

"Where were you when I needed you?" This from my son of sixty now, still a wounded child within. Steven. He who feels I deserted him emotionally when he was a young child.

What I don't say is: "I was there for you. You may not remember."

And what I don't say is: You were a difficult baby and child that grew into a difficult man. From the day you were born.

Perhaps we never bonded the way we should have. You

weighing just three pounds in an incubator behind thick glass walls and me going home without you and coming everyday for one month to watch you.

Until one day you were in my arms. I was so ready for you. You moved, you squeaked, you cried and I held you close to my heart and I also cried.

And what I do not say: as you grew older you were prone to tantrums and walking along the back of the couch until you fell off.

And what I do not say: who took you to child psychologists to help me fix your tantrums, your constant crying and your hyper-active personality?

And what I do not say: who sat by your bedside and waited for word about your surgery? Lengthening your leg muscles so you wouldn't walk on your toes.

Who held you night after night while you struggled through asthma attacks?

And what I do not say: who did you call when you left your wife and ran off with a girl half your age? Your wife did not deserve that!

And what I have said: I will always love you. My heart and my door will always be open if you wish to come home.

———

It's these life experiences I want to share with younger women. You may not recall Betty Crocker or even Betty Friedan, but the experiences I went through echo in the stories of women of all ages, even today. What is your two Bettys story?

Everyone has a story. This one is mine.

I Got Here!

Written during the Kitchen Table writer's group

W/here I am today, in this room, writing my life. Sharing my core with writing friends I trust and who trust me. All driven to share our lives, loves, expectations and regrets, and a past that led to our futures. Yes. I understand now. You need to go back to see where you were to appreciate where you are going.

I am here at last. Me, Alice with three names. Rahmey, Borodkin, Brodsky. But I only use one at a time. Rahmey my first name and who I am and always will be; Borodkin, husband of forty-seven years; and Brodsky, new husband of fifteen years. Identity crisis solved!

Here at last. Sharing this moment, this table, this chair, this precious time, writing about my life. I am surprised at getting here, but happy that I learned to follow my gut that has been telling me for years: write your stories!

I think of a passage from Longfellow's A Psalm of Life, "In the world's broad field of battle, in the bivouac of life, be not like dumb driven cattle. Be a hero in the strife!"

I first heard that poem when I was about eight or nine as my dad would read Longfellow to me before I went to bed. It stuck in my brain even though I didn't quite get it at the time. But life can be a battle ground, and I discovered I did not have to follow along the usual path.

Getting here in my life—can't believe that I'm this age—surprises me as I look at accomplishments that sound like someone else's life! I had no idea I was a rebel. I was not a hero in the strife. I was a wife of the 1960s. I cleaned and cleaned the house, I cooked and I had 2.3 children like The Good Wife Book said I should.

However, as I look back, I didn't know that I couldn't, and shouldn't, be that hero in the poem.

I didn't know I shouldn't learn to fly a plane or enjoy the amazing freedom it gave to me as I controlled my life and my destiny! A door opened and I flew right through it to this chair at this table, with these friends, my pen and a story of my life!

Acknowledgments

I had always thought, since I was writing the book and it was my memoir, I had only myself to thank. Not the case.

I must thank Anne Randolph, our fearless leader of Kitchen Table Writing. She saw something I didn't as I was writing my essays about my life: a book. Thank you, Anne, for your friendship and encouragement throughout the years.

And thank you to my writing family. These are the women who, every Wednesday morning, join me around Anne's big kitchen table. They have created a safe place to write our deepest, most hidden thoughts…from the heart and the gut. We never know if we will pass the Kleenex for laughter or tears.

And of course, Mr. Wonderful. Thank you to my husband, Arnold Brodsky, who from the beginning thought my writing was more than good. His support throughout this journey allowed me to move in directions I never thought possible.

They are not here now, but I want to thank my parents as well. Ruth Rahmey, Mama the Diva, and Moe Rahmey—the best entrepreneur, marketer and salesman I have ever known. Thanks for all the beautiful things you both taught me. Some good and sometimes not so good.

And of course all the Borodkins, but especially Mina and Abe. Their music and stories of Russia and coming to America made many memories that are now committed to paper.

I still ponder about my first husband, Howard Borodkin, who played such a large part in my life story. Where would we be so many years later if he had lived longer? Thanks, Howard, for the forty-seven years we did have. And thanks for opening the doors to flight that allowed me to fly through to my future.

Thanks for the memories, Gottlieb family! Grandma Esther and Grandpa Max. Esther's recipes and Max's driving lessons at 13. And so much hugging and kissing. Never doubted for a minute how much you both loved me.

And the rest of my beloved Rahmeys—Grandma Sophia and Grandpa Eli. Thanks for sharing and making me proud of my heritage. The Arabic lessons, the coffee, the recipes, the lessons learned about business. Your love meant so much. And thanks to all the cousins on both sides and all the stories that made up the fabric of my life.

Thank you to my sister Ellen just for being you. The only one who remembers some of the stories I share in this book. Someday I hope she writes her story as she looks back on her life. Even though we are eleven years apart, we still have our shared moments. And thanks, Ellen, for being an inspiration for me to follow my own path as you have followed yours.

A warm and special thanks to my daughter and friend Julie. What a treat to have you in my life. As you grow older we grow closer. We have shared many life events. Some good and some troubling. Thanks for being there and part of my life.

And Steven, my first child. Blond and blue-eyed, but it seems always troubled.

I will remind him that my heart and door will always be open for him should he want to come home.

What would I do without my editor and friend, Barbara Munson? Who but she could take so many essays and make them flow into a book? And who but Barb could show me that this was more then a memoir, but a lesson for future generations. Who encouraged me to show my vulnerable side?

And thank you to Nick Zelinger. Artist extraordinaire. He saw my vision for a book cover. He got it! He was the one who said, "Some rebels wear pearls"!

This entire book is not just mine. It is a collaborative effort of memories, people here and people no longer with us, editor, book designer, and friends who have their own stories. Thank you, all.

Nemo and Alice

About the Author

Alice Borodkin's past struggle to be validated for who she was during the rise of feminism sets an example and life lesson for younger women today. Her new memoir, *Caught Between the Bettys*, describes how growing up during the tumultuous 1950's, 60's and 70's propelled her to go after men's jobs and eventually seek political office and work on behalf of women's equality. She describes in her book how she had felt identity-less and torn between being a "good housewife" and being true to herself. Women of the current era may take for granted their equal rights, not realizing the punishing effort it was for women back then to fight for their self-worth.

After her career in business and marketing, both primarily men's jobs at the time, she went on to serve in the Colorado State House for eight years. In that position she took a firm stand on numerous women's issues.

Alice is married to Arnold Brodsky. They live in Denver with their dog, Nemo.

Follow or contact Alice Borodkin at:

Website:
http://www.aliceborodkin.com

Email:
alice@aliceborodkin.com

Facebook Page:
https://www.facebook.com/authoraliceborodkin

LinkedIn:
https://www.linkedin.com/in/aliceborodkinco

CPSIA information can be obtained
at www.ICGtesting.com
Printed in the USA
FSOW02n0125290915
11516FS